THE
ORIGAMI
WORKSHOP

D1360237

THE ORIGAMI WORKSHOP

Gay Merrill Gross

Photography by Nancy Palubniak
Illustrations by Katherine Fuetsch

A FRIEDMAN/FAIRFAX BOOK

Library of Congress Cataloging-in-Publication Data

Gross, Gay Merrill.
   [Art of origami]
   The origami workshop / Gay Merrill Gross; photography by
Nancy Palubniak ; illustrations by Kathryne Fuetsch.
     p.   cm.
   Originally published under title: Art of origami.
   Includes index.
   ISBN 1-56799-148-3 (pbk.)
   1. Origami.   I. Title.
TT870.G78   1995
736'.982—dc20
                                     94-26921
                                      CIP

Editors: Nathaniel Marunas and Kelly Matthews
Art Director: Jeff Batzli
Designer: Patrick McCarthy
Photography Editors: Daniella Jo Nilva and Christopher C. Bain

Originally published as *The Art of Origami*

Typeset by Bookworks Plus
Color separations by Universal Color Scanning, Ltd.
Printed in China by Leefung-Asco Printers Ltd.

For bulk purchases and special sales, please contact:
Friedman/Fairfax Publishers
Attention: Sales Department
15 West 26th Street
New York, NY 10010
212/685-6610 FAX 212/685-1307

DEDICATION

This book is dedicated to Lillian Oppenheimer (1898–1992), the "First Lady of Origami," and to all of my origami friends.

ACKNOWLEDGMENTS

This book represents a collection not only of original origami models but also of creative ideas, all generously shared. When Lillian Oppenheimer founded The Origami Center of America, her desire to share and spread origami set the tone and spirit that has promoted such a free exchange among paperfolders.

Thank you to all who have contributed designs, creative ideas, and other assistance in the production of this book.

For original origami designs: Paolo Bascetta, Didier Boursin, Sam Ciulla, Gloria Farison, Thomas Hull, Humiaki Huzita, Rachel Katz, Kenneth Kawamura, Yoshihide Momotani, Ralph Matthews, Lillian Oppenheimer (on behalf of Molly Kahn), Vicente Palacios and Mrs. France (on behalf of Adolfo Cerceda), Aldo Putignano, Robert Neale, Nick Robinson, Beatrice Rohm (on behalf of Fred Rohm), Lewis Simon, and Mike Thomas.

For introducing me to new origami designs used in this book: Laura Kruskal, Shirley Johannesma, Ruthanne Bessman, Dorothy Kaplan, Hisa Amimoto, deg farrelly, Doris Ruth Oppenheimer, Mimi Hug, Eiki Momotani, Eriko Momotani, Pearl Chin, Megan Hicks, and Alice Gray.

For ideas on paper decorating techniques: Mike Thomas (webbing), Doris Ruth Oppenheimer (rubber stamps), and Mark Kennedy (paper painting).

For research material: Mark Kennedy, Michael Shall, David Lister, and Laura Kruskal.

Credit and thanks go to the following people for contributing creative ideas: Megan Hicks (Diamond Decoration barrettes), Pearl Chin (Corsage), Anne McDonald (garland of Lucky Stars), Kathryn Rahnfeld (finger notches on *masu* box cover), Ray Blackburn (*masu* box modular cube), Kathleen O'Regan (folding a *masu* box without center creases), Bob Brill (hiding color inside Butterfly Ball), Thoki Yenn (using a shallow box to assemble Butterfly Ball), and Jean Baden-Gillette (jewelry construction).

A special thank you to Pearl Chin for all her generous help and to John Blackman who designed many of the useful items for the Crane, Hexahedron, and Fluted Diamond models, and loaned us some of his creations for photographing.

The traditional Japanese *noshi* and *go-hei* were generously loaned by Lore Schirokauer.

Paper Sources: Kotobuki Trading Company, San Francisco, California; Sopp America, Inc., Dayton, New Jersey; and A Thousand Cranes, New York, New York.

I would also like to thank the creative staff at Michael Friedman Publishing: Kelly Matthews and Nathaniel Marunas (Editors), Jeff Batzli (Art Director), Kathryne Fuetsch (Illustrator), Patrick McCarthy (Book Designer), and Nancy Palubniak (Photographer).

For additional assistance: Bernice Smith, V'Ann Cornelius, Kathleen Devine, Rosaly Evnine, Rachel Katz, and Tony Cheng.

Thank you to my mother who not only handed me my first origami book at age nine, but has encouraged my fascination with folded paper ever since.

My own knowledge and education in the folding arts are enhanced by my many wonderful associations and friendships made through The Friends of the Origami Center of America. Thank you to Michael Shall, who founded this forum for folders, and to Lillian Oppenheimer, whose generous and sharing nature has laid the foundation for many organizations around the world devoted to paperfolding.

TABLE OF CONTENTS

ORIGAMI: A HISTORICAL OVERVIEW

Part III
PAPERS AND SPECIAL TECHNIQUES 114

ORIGAMI: A HISTORICAL OVERVIEW

A folk art, a creative art, a mathematical puzzle, a game—all of these terms can be used to describe origami. Some people are attracted to origami for its simplicity, while others marvel at the minds of the people who are able to devise the patterns for some of the ingenious creations. Some look to origami as a way of entertaining, while others find it has a calming, relaxing effect.

Origami is unique among papercrafts in that it requires no materials other than the paper itself. Cutting, gluing, or drawing on the paper is avoided, using only folds to create the desired result. No special skills or artistic talent are needed for origami, although a good amount of patience and perseverance are very helpful. Models can be made by following instructions exactly or by varying the folds to create something a little different. Experimenting with the paper may also lead you to design a totally new, original paperfold.

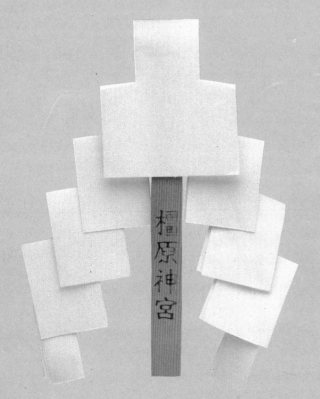

The importance of the *go-hei* in the Shinto religion illustrates the reverence the Japanese give to the qualites of pure white paper.

The word *origami* comes from the Japanese language. *Ori* means folded and *kami* means paper. When the two words are combined, the *k* from *kami* becomes a *g*, giving us *origami*. Paperfolding as a traditional folk art pervaded the Japanese culture more strongly than any other. But traditional paperfolding did not exist in Japan alone, so we will try to go back and trace the roots of paperfolding around the world.

Reconstructing a history of paperfolding is more a matter of conjecture and supposition than of hard facts. It is probable that the art began in China, where papermaking methods were first developed two thousand years ago. Although certain traditional designs such as the junk and pagoda are generally attributed to the Chinese, no records accounting for the time or place of their creation can confirm this or tell us just how old these folds are. Evidence of paperfolding in China is often associated with the Chinese tradition of re-creating small objects used during a person's life and then burying or burning them with a deceased person. This practice of funerary folds is still carried out today in areas strongly influenced by Chinese religion and culture, such as Hong Kong and Singapore.

Papermaking techniques were not readily shared by the Chinese but did eventually travel to Korea and then Japan by the seventh century. The closely guarded knowledge then spread in the direction of the Arab world, reaching Spain by the twelfth century. During this journey, did simple paperfolding principles spread with the knowledge of making the paper? Or did each country independently discover that paper could not only be written and drawn on, but manipulated into forms by creating a pattern of creases? Despite the similarity of some traditional models associated with different paperfolding traditions (the Japanese boat with sail and the Spanish *pajarita*, for example), most people believe that there was little commingling of paperfolding ideas until the end of the nineteenth century.

THE JAPANESE TRADITION

The Japanese have always had a reverence for the special qualities of paper. Even the Japanese word for paper, *kami*, is pronounced identically (although the characters are written differently) as their word for God. For more than a thousand years, paper has played a prominent part in the Shinto religion. Streamers of white paper cut

In Spain the *pajarita* (little bird) is as widely recognized as the paper airplane is in America.

into a zigzag pattern are called *o-shide*, or *go-hei* when found in pairs. *O-shide* are placed at the entrances to Shinto shrines, while *go-hei* are found in a place of honor inside the shrine, denoting the presence of the deity.

The first Japanese paperfolds did not seek to create the likeness of any living or material object but were merely abstract, decorative forms used for ceremonial purposes. These early paperfolds, believed to date back to the twelfth century, are folded ornaments called *noshi*. A noshi is attached to a package to signify that it is a gift (serving the same purpose as a bow in Western culture). It also symbolizes a wish for the recipient's good fortune. The standardized manner for folding noshi involved pleating the paper at prescribed, irregular angles, not an easy task. Etiquette required that young women be skilled in folding noshi. It has been theorized that simple, representational paperfolds that would appeal to children evolved as a way of exercising young fingers. This would give them practice in working with paper and help to develop the manual skills needed to fold the more intricate and difficult patterns of the noshi. The custom of attaching a noshi to a gift still continues today, but it is rare to find someone folding their own noshi. Commercially made noshi are now available in Japanese stores, or wrapping paper can be purchased that has a noshi pattern on it.

In 1845, a volume in a Japanese collection called the *Kan-no-mado* showed drawings and some sketchy diagrams for making more than forty folded figures known at that time. This publication, one of the earliest to record the folding pattern for an origami model, shows that origami had reached a stage of greater intricacy and broader scope than the folding of the decorative noshi or simple toylike figures. It also shows us that the rules of traditional Japanese origami did not prohibit the use of slits in or drawings on the paper.

WESTERN TRADITION

The most well-known and possibly the oldest paperfold in Europe is an abstract design of a small bird (*pajarita*) that originated in Spain but was known to a lesser extent throughout Europe. In France, the design was a hen, in Germany, a crow, and in England, a hobbyhorse.

Evidence of the popularity of the pajarita can be found in its occasional appearance in late-nineteenth-century drawings and paintings. But this traditional paperfold was probably known much earlier than that. The same creases used for folding the pajarita are found in folded baptismal certificates that date back to eighteenth-century Germany. By the mid-nineteenth century, there were quite a few decorative and playful paperfolds known in Europe, many of them based on the same folding pattern as the pajarita. During this period, German educator Friedrich Froebel, who founded the kindergarten based on his philosophy that children learn from play, promoted paperfolding as a learning exercise for children.

Several traditional Western folds were neither handed down from mother to child as in Japan nor taught in a formal educational setting. These "playground folds" were taught by one child to another. The paper airplane, the newspaper hat, and the fortune-teller, or cootie catcher, are all examples of traditional Western paperfolds.

In both the East and the West, paperfolding experienced a transition from ceremonial to playful folds to use in education, and finally to its present status as a creative art and craft.

CREATIVE PAPERFOLDING

One of the first persons to experiment creatively with paperfolding was Spanish philosopher Miguel de Unamuno (1864–1936). Although some of his designs were published, they reached a very limited audience. Their main influence was in promoting the idea of creative folding among the folders of Spain. Several of these people eventually migrated to Argentina around the time of the Spanish civil war (1936) and continued this creative approach there.

Far more influential were the explorations of some of the Japanese folders of the early twentieth century. Most important among them was Akira Yoshizawa. Yoshizawa, who was born in 1911, has devoted a lifetime to origami. His designs, techniques, and use of paper all represent the work of an artist and creative genius. Fortunately, his work did not remain known only in Japan. Through contacts with the West, he has had many exhibitions of his work in Europe and the United States, special classes have been organized, and most important, his designs have been made available for other folders in the dozen or so books he has written.

Almost as important as Yoshizawa's advances in creative folding is the diagramming system he developed that uses easily understood symbols. This symbol notation was adopted with some modifications by authors Robert Harbin and Samuel Randlett and used in their classic books *The Art of Origami* (Randlett, 1961) and *Secrets of Origami* (Harbin, 1964). They have subsequently become the standard symbols for origami books written around the world. This internationally understood symbol notation makes it possible to follow the pictorial explanations for folding a model even if the text is written in a language you don't understand. Publishing a new origami design today means that it can be immediately shared with an international community. What a difference from the early years in our paper history, when it took more than a thousand years for papermaking techniques to spread from China to Europe.

Today, origami is an international creative pastime. Building upon the basics of the traditional Eastern and Western designs, many folders around the world have followed the creative path of leaders such as Yoshizawa and Unamuno and are devising their own new designs. The repertoire of a couple hundred traditional folds that existed at the beginning of the twentieth century has grown in the latter half of the twentieth century to tens of thousands of new designs with an endless number yet to be discovered.

One of the reasons for origami's change from a relatively static, traditional folk art to an ever-changing creative art was the increased availability of paper. The first model for a papermaking machine was created in Europe in 1798. Up until that time, every sheet was created by hand, one at a time. With that in mind, it makes sense that paperfolding as a leisurely activity did not catch hold in a big way until paper became less expensive and available in greater supply. Another reason was the ability to record folding instructions in books. This meant that paperfolding designs were no longer limited to a few simple figures a mother could memorize and then teach to a young child.

The first records of paperfolding were drawings of finished figures with no explanation of how to make them. Just as the pajarita appeared in drawings and paintings in Europe, so did the crane, or *tsuru*, in Japan. At least one or two Japanese books that show folding methods predate the *Kan-no-mado* of 1845. One of these was called *Sembazuru Orikata* (*Folding a Thousand Cranes*), which was published in 1797. This book showed how to fold families of multiple connected cranes from single sheets of paper cut into a series of connecting squares.

The occasional book on paperfolding started appearing in English in the first half of the twentieth century. These books, such as Murray and Rigney's *Paperfolding for Fun*, were all comprised of traditional models. The first book in English to suggest that origami could be a

The *noshi* is an example of Japanese ceremonial folding. (From the collection of Lore Schirokauer.)

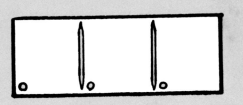

creative art was Robert Harbin's *Paper Magic*, first published in England in 1956. Harbin, a South African–born stage magician living in England, was fortunate to have contact with Ligia Montoya and the Japanese origami master Akira Yoshizawa. Montoya lived in Argentina and was a disciple of Unamuno's school of Spanish folding. Their influence on Harbin was reflected in the many books Harbin wrote on origami, which in turn influenced hundreds of paperfolders, many of whom eventually contacted the author. One such person was a fifty-eight-year-old woman in New York City who enjoyed making things with her hands although she had never thought she was particularly good at it. The success she had with paperfolding delighted her so much that she could not understand why everyone in the world would not want to learn this remarkable activity. Lillian Oppenheimer began collecting every model and book on origami she could find at the time. The new models she learned she taught to others and encouraged them to teach as well. Her enthusiasm and desire to learn and share more led her in 1958 to found the Origami Center of America. By creating a forum for bringing folders together, the cross-fertilization of creative ideas has increased the depth and appeal of this art. What was originally considered a children's activity was now attracting the interest of mathematicians, engineers, scientists, computer programmers, college professors, and professional artists.

The Origami Center offered classes and meetings for paperfolders. They held annual conventions, published a newsletter, and sold origami books and paper. In later years, many other countries followed Lillian Oppenheimer's example and started their own origami societies. In 1980, The Friends of The Origami Center of America was founded by paperfolder Michael Shall to continue Lillian Oppenheimer's origami activities. Today, the Friends (now called Origami USA) has a membership of almost two thousand paperfolders around the world.

The models in this book represent the international nature of origami today. Creators from the United States, England, France, Italy, Japan, and Argentina have all contributed designs. The models also represent origami's past and present. From the past are several classic designs that were favorites more than one hundred years ago and have lasted to become even more well known and appealing in present times. From the multitude of modern designs, those presented here offer examples of some of the popular themes in origami today, such as action toys, practical origami, and modulars (constructions of several interlocking units). But most important, the models in this book were chosen for their ability to delight and fascinate both the folder and those with whom they share their art. Hopefully, you also will be enchanted and inspired by these designs' charm and ingenuity.

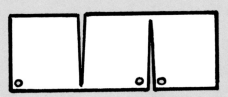

Published in 1797 *Sembazuru Orikata* (*Folding a Thousand Cranes*) showed how to make families of cranes such as these. Slits are cut in the paper as shown. The circle indicates where the head is folded.

11

Part I

How to Read Origami Diagrams

ORIGAMI SYMBOLS

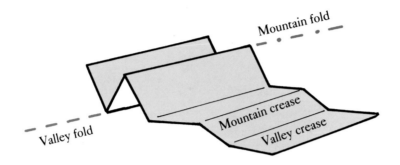

Mountain fold

Valley fold

Mountain crease

Valley crease

VALLEY FOLD:

Fold the paper forward.

When you open paper that has been valley-folded, you will see a concave crease that bends inward like a groove or valley. This is called a valley crease.

MOUNTAIN FOLD:

Fold the paper backward.

When you open paper that has been mountain-folded, you will see a convex crease that bends outward—it has a peak that you can pinch. This is called a mountain crease.

Fold toward you (valley fold) and in the direction of the arrow.

Fold away from you (mountain fold) and in the direction of the arrow.

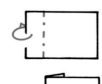

Fold and unfold.

MOUNTAIN AND VALLEY FOLD:

Train your paper to go both ways by folding the crease as both a valley and a mountain fold.

Turn the model over.

Insert.

Unfold.

Repeat steps 6 through 8 here.

An X-ray line allows you to see through the paper to an interior line or serves as an imaginary line used as a reference mark.

Hold here.

Match the dots.

Rotate the paper one-quarter turn (the top of the model will rotate to the side).

Push here.

90° Form a right angle.

Raw Edge

Crease

Back Layer

Front Layer

Repeat here.

Folded Edge

Double Raw Edge

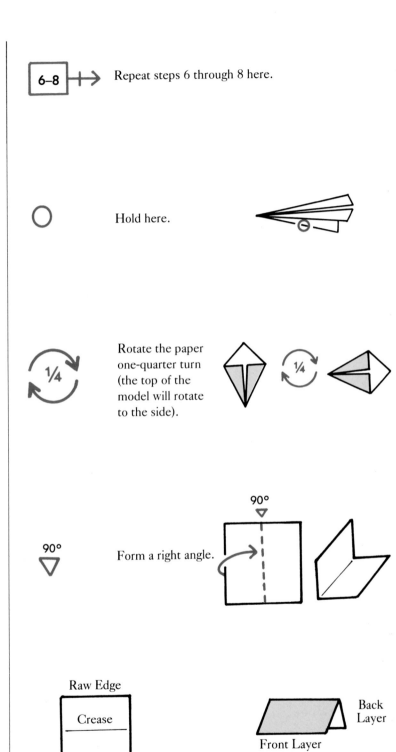
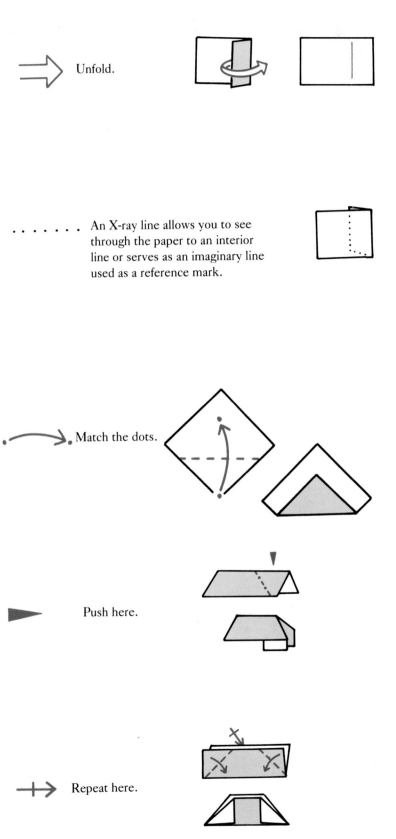

BASIC FOLDS

Folding patterns that are commonly used in origami are given easy-to-remember names based on what they look like when the folds are completed.

BOOK FOLD

Fold one side edge to the opposite edge.

ICE-CREAM-CONE FOLD

Fold two adjacent sides inward to meet at the center.

DIAPER FOLD

Fold one corner to the opposite corner.

HOUSE-ROOF FOLD

Fold two adjacent corners inward to meet at the center.

CUPBOARD FOLD

Fold two opposite sides inward to meet at the center.

BLINTZ FOLD

Fold all four corners inward to meet at the center.

Note: Although less easily recognizable, the crease pattern for a sideways book fold is still called a book fold. The same is true for all the basic folds.

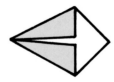

Still an ice-cream-cone fold

Still a book fold

Still a cupboard fold

BASIC TECHNIQUES

Almost every origami model beyond the beginner's level uses one or
more of these basic techniques. It is a good idea to practice them on scrap paper
before folding them on an actual model.

REVERSE FOLDS

A reverse fold requires two layers of paper
connected by a folded edge or spine.

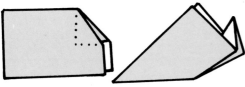

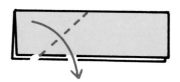

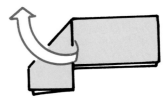

INSIDE REVERSE FOLD

This process involves *reversing* an end or corner of the paper so that it lies *inside* the model, sandwiched in between the front and back layers. The end that is reversed may be totally buried inside the model or it may stick out at the side.

1 You may wish to prepare your paper first by making a simple valley fold that will serve as a precrease.

2 Check to be sure that this is the shape you would like the paper to ultimately take, then make a supersharp crease. Unfold the crease and smooth it flat. (Mountain-fold and unfold on the same crease if you wish.)

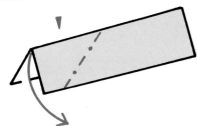

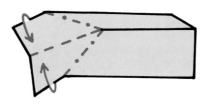

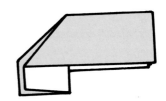

3 Spread the layers of your paper apart. Apply pressure (push in) at the mountain-folded edge (spine) until it changes to a valley fold. At the same time, the precreases you made earlier will both become mountain-folded edges.

4 This shows the inside reverse fold in progress. Begin to flatten your paper into the position shown in the next drawing.

5 The inside reverse fold is complete. Try folding the inside reverse folds illustrated before step 1.

OUTSIDE REVERSE FOLD

This process involves wrapping an end of the double layer around the outside of the paper.

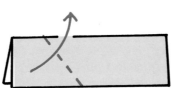

1 Make a precrease by folding the end of the paper toward the spine or folded edge.

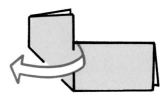

2 Check to make sure that this is the shape you would like the paper to ultimately take, then make a supersharp crease and unfold. (Mountain-fold and unfold on the same crease if you wish.)

15

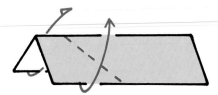

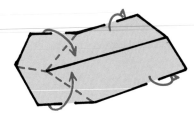

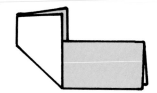

3 Separate the front and back layers of the paper. Folding along the precreases, wrap the end around the outside of the model (like turning up a cuff on a sleeve).

4 This shows the outside reverse fold in progress; your model should follow the crease pattern shown in the drawing. Flatten all layers and . . .

5 . . . your outside reverse fold is complete.

SQUASH FOLD

This is one example of a squash fold. In general, a flap is opened to form a pocket and then squashed flat. Try the following on a practice sheet book-folded in half.

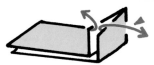

3 Separate the raw edges and insert a finger deep into the pocket to open it wide. Push down on the folded edge.

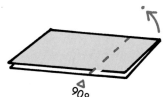

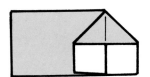

1 Make a precrease.

2 Lift the flap so that it stands straight up.

4 Flatten the pocket evenly so that the crease line that was the folded edge aligns with the edges below it.

RABBIT EAR

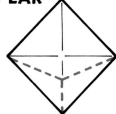

A rabbit ear is a procedure in which a corner of paper is pinched in half to form a protruding point, or "rabbit ear." The crease pattern for this move takes the form of the letter Y. Notice that within a triangular-shaped area, each crease bisects (divides in two) an angle of the triangle. Here is an example of a rabbit ear. Try it on a square of practice paper folded in half along both diagonals (two diaper folds).

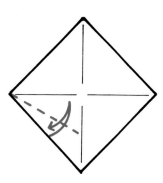

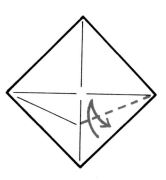

1 Bring the lower left edge to the horizontal centerline. Make a partial fold: Crease only from the far left corner to the vertical centerline. Unfold.

2 Repeat step 1 on the lower right edge.

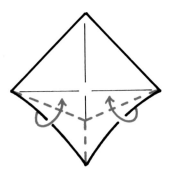 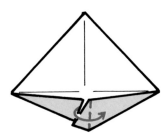 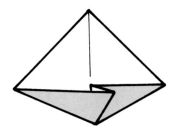

3 Pinch the bottom corner in half. At the same time, refold on the creases you made in steps 1 and 2.

4 Your rabbit ear is complete. Sometimes the point is left standing up, but usually you are told to flip it to one side, . . .

5 . . . flattening it to this position.

BASES

Many origami models begin with the same sequence of folds. These beginning steps have been classified into bases that are usually named after a traditional model that begins with that combination of folds.

The most common of all paperfolds is probably the fan. The alternating valley and mountain folds allow the paper to be collapsed into a pleated pattern. If the alternating valley and mountain folds are arranged in a radial instead of parallel pattern, you have two important origami bases, the preliminary base and the waterbomb base.

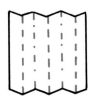

Pleated Fan **Preliminary Base** **Waterbomb Base**

PRELIMINARY BASE

The preliminary base is the foundation of thousands of origami models, as well as the preliminary stage of the bird and frog bases.

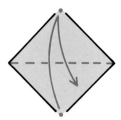 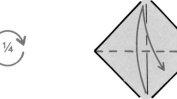

1 Begin with the colored side facing up.
DIAPER FOLD and UNFOLD: Bring the bottom point up to the top point. Crease and unfold.

2 Rotate your paper so that the crease you made in step 1 is now vertical.
DIAPER FOLD and UNFOLD: Fold the square in half along the other diagonal. Crease and unfold.

3 Turn over to the white side.
BOOK FOLD and UNFOLD: Bring the bottom edge up to the top edge, folding the square in half. Unfold and rotate your paper so that the crease you just made is vertical.

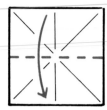

4 BOOK FOLD: Fold the square in half. Leave this fold in place. The folded edge should be at the top.

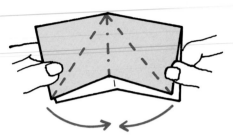

5 Grasp the sides of the paper and hold it in the air. Push your hands together slightly so that the bottom raw edges separate and move away from each other. Continue pushing your hands together until they meet and . . .

6 . . . you see four flaps extending from a central axis. Pair two flaps together on the right and two flaps together on the left, flattening your paper to . . .

WATERBOMB BASE

The Waterbomb is a traditional origami model that inflates to form a Paper Balloon. The beginning sequence of folds that form this model are known as the waterbomb base.

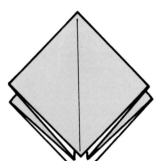

7 . . . a diamond-shaped square. This is your finished preliminary base.

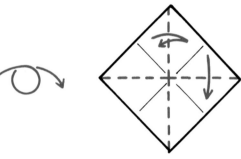

1 Begin with the colored side facing up. BOOK FOLD and UNFOLD (two times): Fold and unfold the square in half in both directions. Then turn the open paper over to the white side.

2 On the white side, diaper-fold the square in half and unfold. Then diaper-fold in the other direction and leave this fold in place.

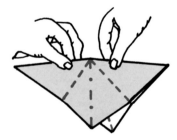

3 Grasp the paper at the top folded edge and hold it in the air. Push your hands together slightly so that the two bottom points separate and move away from each other. Continue pushing your hands together until . . .

4 . . . you see a star shape with four flaps extending from a central axis. Pair two flaps together on the right and two flaps together on the left, flattening your paper into . . .

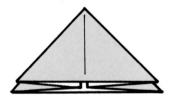

5 . . . a triangular shape. This is your finished waterbomb base. If you look under the bottom edge, you will see the hidden layers of paper.

COMPARING THE PRELIMINARY AND WATERBOMB BASES

If you unfold the preliminary and waterbomb bases, you will see that the crease patterns are identical. Only the color instructions and the final "push" into position are different.

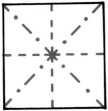
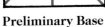
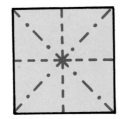

Preliminary Base　　　**Waterbomb Base**

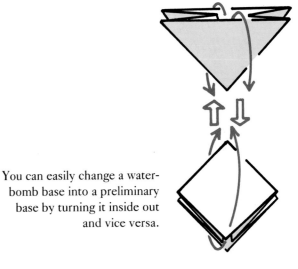

You can easily change a water-bomb base into a preliminary base by turning it inside out and vice versa.

BIRD BASE

The bird base forms the beginning of two classic origami models, the Crane and the Flapping Bird. But the usefulness of this base is not limited to birds alone. It has been used for creating hundreds of other models of every type.

1 Begin with a preliminary base (see page 17). Make sure the open end is pointing toward you.
ICE-CREAM-CONE FOLD (front and back):

Fold up the lower edge of the right flap (front layer only) so that the double raw edge lies along the vertical centerline. Repeat on the left, then turn over and repeat on the back.

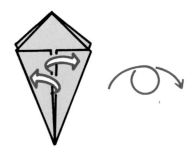

2 Open the cone flaps on the front. Then turn the model over.

3 Mountain-fold the top point backward along the top edge of the "cone." (The ice cream disappears.)

4 Open the cone flaps.

5 In one hand, grasp single point A, the bottom corner of the front layer. As you lift A upward, hold the points below it in your other hand. Continue lifting A up as far as it will go to form . . .

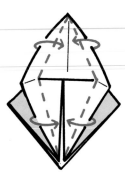 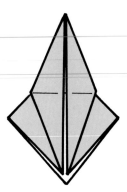 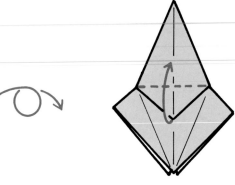

6 . . . a boat shape. Beginning at the bottom, bring the raw edges together. Make sure the top and bottom points are neatly folded. Sharpen the folds of the long diamond shape.

7 Turn the model over.

8 Lift up the small triangular flap as far as it will go.

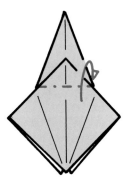 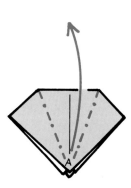 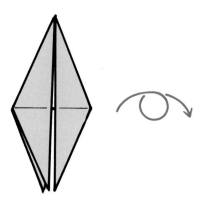

9 Mountain-fold the small and tall triangular flaps to the back of the model, along the existing crease.

10 Repeat steps 5 and 6 on this side.

11 Turn the model over.

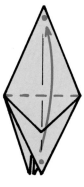 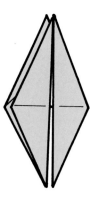

12 Lift the single bottom point up to the top (the small triangular flap will also flip upward).

13 You now have a double diamond shape with a small triangular flap sandwiched in between the front and back layers. This is your finished bird base.

FOLDING HINTS

• For accurate folding, match edges and corners as neatly and as carefully as you can. Then make a light crease. Check to be sure that the edges still match. If they don't, make a slight adjustment. When everything is neatly aligned, make a sharp crease.

• If you are a beginning folder, try to make your creases as sharp as possible and fold on a hard, smooth surface.

• If a step is unclear, look ahead to the next drawing. This will tell you what shape you wish to form as a result of the step you are working on.

• It is usually easier to fold paper by lifting the edge or corner near you and bringing it to the edge or corner away from you. The result is a horizontal crease. Avoid making vertical creases unless there is already an existing crease there.

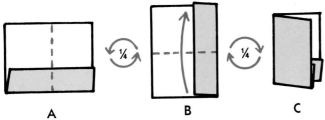

A   B   C

• If a drawing indicates a vertical fold such as in drawing A, it is a good idea to rotate your paper one-quarter turn and make the horizontal fold (drawing B), then reposition your paper so that it appears exactly as it would had you made the original vertical fold (drawing C).

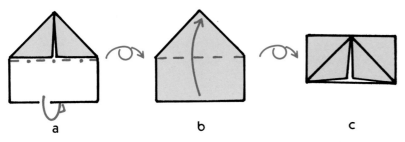

a   b   c

• It is usually easier to make a valley fold than it is to make a mountain fold. If a drawing indicates a mountain fold (drawing a), you can turn your paper over to the back side and make a valley fold on the back (drawing b). When you return your paper to the front, you will have the desired mountain fold (drawing c).

• It is easier to see the edges of your paper if you fold on a surface of a color that contrasts with the colors on both sides of your paper. If it doesn't, simply place a suitably colored sheet of paper on top of your folding surface.

MODEL RATING

The models are rated according to their level of difficulty as follows:

★ **Very easy**
★★ **Easy**
★★★ **Intermediate**
★★★★ **Challenging**

Part II

MODELS
Tricks and Toys

SHIRT AND PANTS

Design by Rachel Katz (Smithtown, New York, USA)

Rachel Katz is the founder of LIFE (Long Island Folding Enthusiasts). Her forte is teaching origami and combining it with clever stories. This adaptation of the traditional shirt model is unique in that the shirt features a bottom slit for inserting pants or a skirt. This delightful model is very appealing folded from colorful paper. Or folded from money, it can be given as a gift.

★

PAPER:

One rectangle in the proportion 2:1 (half a square) for the Shirt and a rectangle of equal size for the Pants.

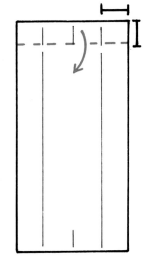

SHIRT:

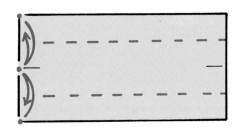

1 Begin with the colored side of your rectangle facing up. Pinch the center of each short side of your rectangle.

2 CUPBOARD FOLD and UNFOLD: Fold the long sides inward to meet at the center, using your pinch marks as a guide. Crease and unfold.

3 Turn your paper over to the white side and position it so that the short sides are at the top and bottom. At the top edge, fold down a colored hem equal in width or slightly narrower than one cupboard door flap.

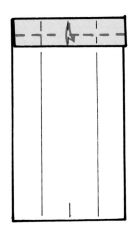

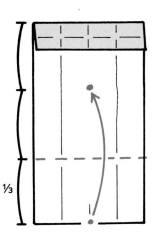

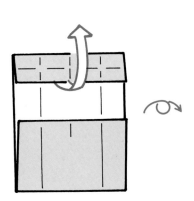

4 Take the raw edge of the hem and bring it up to the folded edge. Crease and unfold.

5 Fold the bottom edge up one-third the height of the figure. (Check to make sure your one-third fold is accurate and adjust it if necessary.)

6 Unfold the hem so the top edge is a raw edge again. Then turn your model over to the colored side.

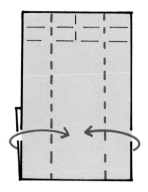 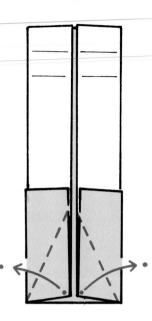 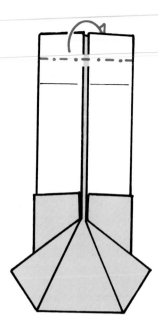

7 CUPBOARD FOLD: Fold the longer sides inward to meet at the center. You are folding along existing creases.

8 Lift the loose corners at the center of the bottom edge and spread them apart. (Notice in the drawing where the slanted folds you are making start and end.)

9 Your figure should now look like this. Mountain-fold the top edge to the back, along the existing crease that is the closest to the top edge.

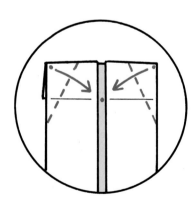 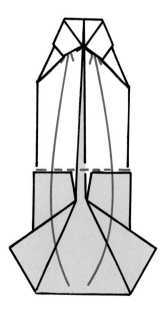 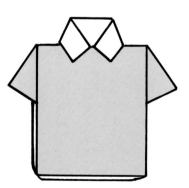

10 Fold the top corners down and inward to meet at the intersection of the horizontal crease and the vertical centerline. You are forming the Shirt's collar.

11 Lift the bottom edge up and slide it under the points of the collar as far as it will comfortably go. Crease firmly at the new bottom edge of your Shirt.

12 Here is your completed Shirt. Notice the opening at the bottom of the Shirt. This is where you will insert the Pants.

Variations:

You can vary the look of your shirt by adding a white border to the bottom of the Shirt and the sleeves.

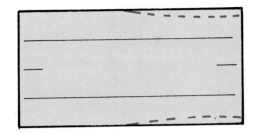

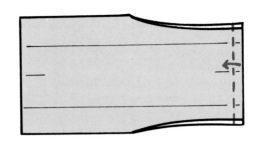

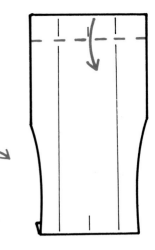

1 Follow steps 1 and 2 for the Shirt. The colored side of your paper is still facing up.

2 To form a border on the sleeves: On half of each of the long edges, fold in a very narrow, tapered hem, as shown in the drawing.

3 To form a border on the Shirt bottom: At the short edge that lies between the hems you just formed, fold in a small hem.

4 Turn your paper over to the all-white side, and continue with step 3 of the Shirt. The hem you just folded in should be at the back side of the bottom edge.

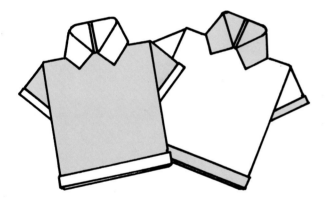

If you would like your Shirt to be white with colored collar and hems, reverse all the color instructions in the diagrams.

This model can also be folded from money. It is not necessary to have your paper be exactly in the proportion 2:1. Follow the original instructions, leaving out the variation that creates a different-colored hem if your currency already has a border printed on it.

PANTS:

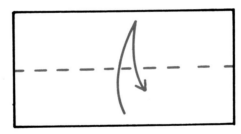

1 BOOK FOLD and UNFOLD: Begin with the white side of your rectangle facing up. Bring the long edges together, folding the paper in half. Crease and unfold.

2 CUPBOARD FOLD: Fold the long sides inward to meet at the center.

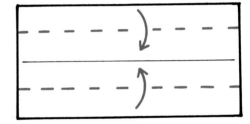

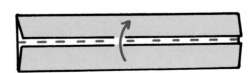

3 Fold the figure in half again, refolding on the existing crease.

4 Fold the short sides toward each other but leave them slightly apart as shown in the next drawing.

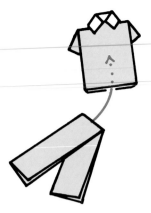

5 Slide the Pants into the opening at the bottom of your Shirt. You can adjust the length of the Pants' legs by sliding the Pants farther in or out until they look right to you.

Variation:
To add a white hem at the bottom of your Pants, begin with the colored side of your paper facing up. Fold a small white hem on each short side of your rectangle. Then turn your paper back to the white side and continue with step 1 of the Pants' instructions.

Experiment with different-colored and -patterned papers to vary the look of your Shirt and Pants. See if you can create a Skirt to go with the Shirt by using a square half the size of the rectangle you used for the Shirt. Combine other origami models as accessories. Use your imagination to create a whole fashion line of coordinated outfits.

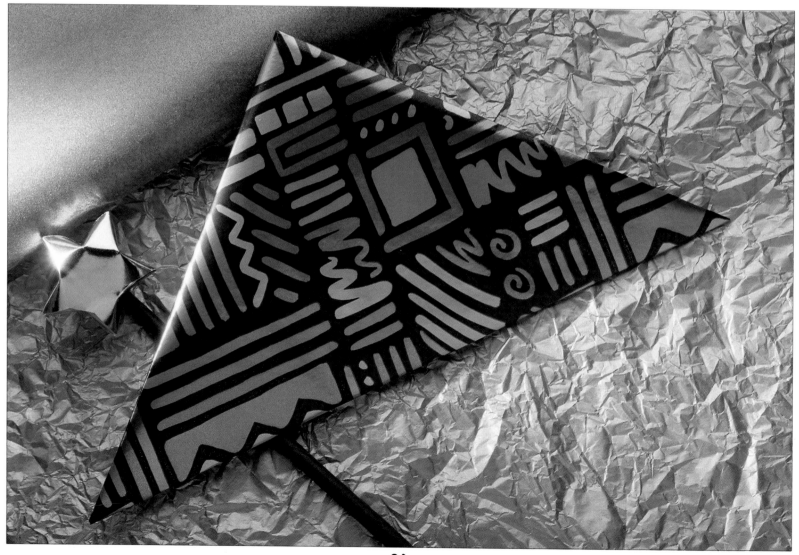

MAGIC POCKET
Traditional Design

This very simple model can be used to perform a magic trick. Flat objects can be made to change their form or disappear!

★
_____
PAPER:

One rectangle in the proportion of 2:1 (half a square), such as 10″ × 5″ (25 × 12.5cm).

PERFORMING THE TRICK:

Secretly fold a one-dollar bill (or any paper currency with a low denomination) and hide it in one pocket. Press that pocket closed. Show the Magic Pocket to your audience. Squeeze open the empty pocket and show them it is empty. Ask to borrow a bill from someone (anything larger than the first bill). Fold it up and insert it in the empty pocket and press it closed. As you talk and move your hand in the air, rotate the model so the other pocket is now facing toward your audience. You can add some magician's flair (or fanfare) such as tapping on the model, blowing on it, or saying a magic word. When you open the pocket, the borrowed bill has turned into a bill worth less money!

In a similar manner, you can transform a piece of colored tissue paper into many smaller pieces (pre-hidden in a pocket) or make whatever flat item you insert disappear.

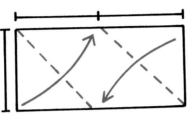

1 Begin with the white side of your rectangle facing up and the long sides at the top and bottom. Fold the left side up to lie along the top edge of your paper. Fold the right side down to lie along the bottom edge.

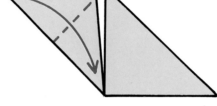

2 Fold the sharp point at the top left down to touch the bottom of the vertical centerline.

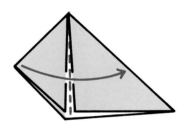

3 Flip the small triangle on the left to the right, folding along the vertical gap.

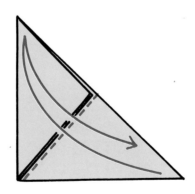

4 Fold the bottom right point up to the top. Your crease will lie along the folded edge that divides the large triangle in half. Crease sharply and unfold.

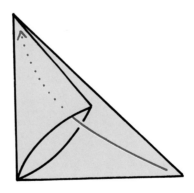

5 Squeeze the smaller, top triangle slightly, causing the double-folded edge to open up into a pocket. Insert the bottom right point into the pocket and slide it in as far as it will go.

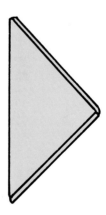

6 Here is your completed model. Notice that your model has two separate and identical pockets. Show only one pocket at a time to your audience so they will not realize there are two.

FLAPPING BIRD

Traditional Design

★★

YOU SHOULD KNOW:

Inside reverse fold

PAPER:

A square of almost any size.

The great appeal of this delightful model has drawn many people under the charm and spell of origami.

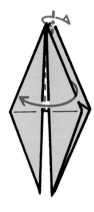 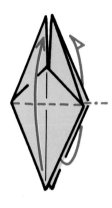 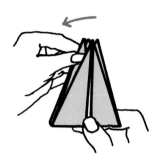 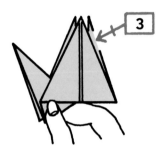

1 Begin with a square folded into a bird base (see page 19). Turn the page: Fold the right-hand flap (front layer only) to the left. Turn over and repeat behind.

2 The wings are at the bottom of the model. Fold the front wing up to the top of the model. Repeat behind.

3 Reach inside (between the wings) and pull out one of the slender inner points and lower it to the position shown in the next drawing.

4 Pinch the base of the slender point to keep it set in this position. Repeat step 3 on the other side.

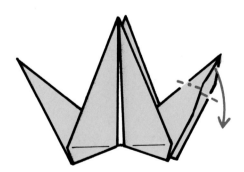 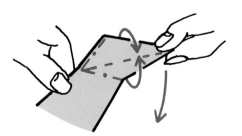 

5 INSIDE REVERSE FOLD: Form the bird's head by making an inside reverse fold at the end of one slender point, as described in the next step.

6 Flatten the tip of the point and pull it downward at an angle. With your other hand, pinch the back of the head to keep it set in this position.

 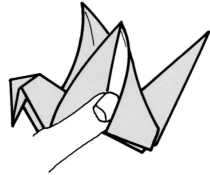

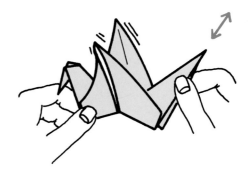

7 Slightly open the pocket at the back half of each wing and gently curve the wings out to the sides. If the flapping action described in the next step gives you trouble, curve the wings farther downward.

8 To make the wings flap: Hold the base of the neck in one hand. Hold the middle of the tail in the other hand. Gently pull the tail away from the body and then release it. Repeat this back-and-forth motion and your Flapping Bird is complete.

DRINKING BIRD

Collected by Laura Kruskal (Princeton, New Jersey, USA)

Here is another action bird model folded from the bird base. During a visit to China, Laura Kruskal learned it from a young woman who was protesting in Tiananmen Square.

★★★

YOU SHOULD KNOW:

Rabbit ear
Inside reverse fold
Squash fold

PAPER:

One square, approximately 6″ (15cm) in size.

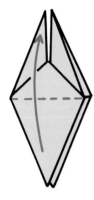

1 Follow Step 1 of the instructions for the Flapping Bird. Fold the bottom point (front layer only) up to the top of the model.

2 RABBIT EAR: On the front layer, individually precrease each of the three folds shown, then pinch the thin top point in half and simultaneously fold down on the other two creases. The rabbit ear that forms should stick straight out from the rest of the model.

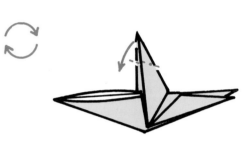

3 Mountain-fold the model in half at the vertical centerline. Rotate the model to the position shown in the next drawing.

4 Inside-reverse-fold the top point to form the bird's head.

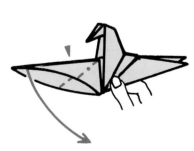

5 Hold the model at the base of the bird's neck. With your other hand, separate the bottom edges of the left point and squash it flat to form a kite shape that points down.

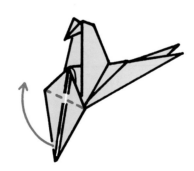

6 Make a soft curve at the widest part of the kite shape, bringing the bottom point out to the left again.

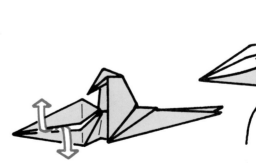

7 Separate the raw edges of the left point, opening the point out to form the bird's drinking container. Shape the container to keep it open.

8 Hold the model as shown, with two fingers of your left hand grasping the inner two layers of the bird, just to the right of the container. Insert the thumb and index finger of your right hand into the pockets slightly behind the bird's neck.

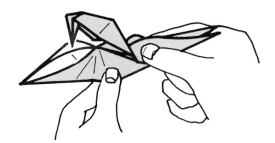

9 Drinking action: Lift your right thumb and index finger and squeeze them together, then return them to their original position. Repeat this motion slowly until you can train your bird to drink a little faster.

Optional: To form a beak, open out the head and pleat the tip toward the back of the head and out again. Then reclose the head.

STELLATED OCTAHEDRON

Design by Sam Ciulla (Tucson, Arizona, USA)

★★
YOU SHOULD KNOW:
Waterbomb base

PAPER:
Almost any size or type of paper
will work.

Sam Ciulla, a professional tennis instructor, has created a paper ball with its own little "kick." The model has an imbalance due to the concentration of paper on the side where the flaps are locked together. This imbalance can turn the model into a roly-poly action toy.

WHAT IS A STELLATED OCTAHEDRON?

Most people know that an octagon is a two-dimensional shape having eight sides. An octahedron is a three-dimensional shape having eight faces. Stellated refers to the fact that each face of the shape points outward instead of being flat, giving it a stellar or starlike appearance.

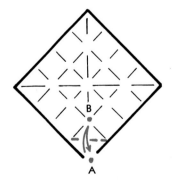

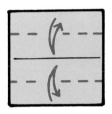

1 Begin with the colored side facing up. BOOK FOLD and UNFOLD: Fold your paper in half and unfold.

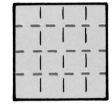

2 CUPBOARD FOLD and UNFOLD: Bring the top and bottom edges to the horizontal centerline. Crease and unfold.

¼

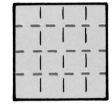

3 Rotate your paper one-quarter turn so that the creases you made are now vertical. Repeat steps 1 and 2 in this direction.

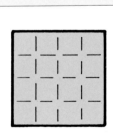

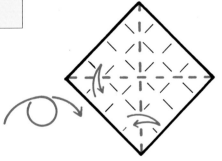

4 Your paper should now be divided into a grid of sixteen little boxes. Turn your paper over to the white side and position it so one corner is near you.

5 DIAPER FOLD and UNFOLD (two times): Bring the bottom corner up to the top corner. Crease and unfold. Rotate your paper one-quarter turn, then crease the other diagonal and unfold.

6 Locate the bottom corner (dot A). Then locate on your grid the nearest intersection of creases (dot B). Fold dot A to dot B. Crease and unfold.

7 Locate the second nearest intersection of creases (dot C), which also happens to be the center point of your paper. Fold dot A to dot C. Crease and unfold.

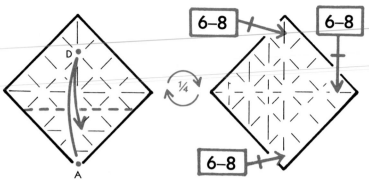
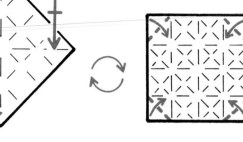
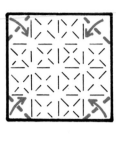
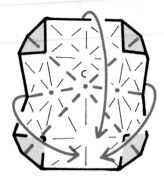

8 Locate the farthest intersection of creases (dot D). Fold dot A to dot D. Crease and unfold.

9 Rotate your paper one-quarter turn. The new bottom corner now becomes dot A. Repeat steps 6 through 8 three more times.

10 The result should be a grid of sixteen little boxes with an **X** in the center of each box. Blunt the corners of your paper by folding each outside corner in along the nearest crease.

11 Press down at C to make sure the center point pops away from you. Raise the sides along the existing mountain folds and push the sides toward each other and down to the center of the bottom edge. Flatten the model. The result is a waterbomb base with blunted corners.

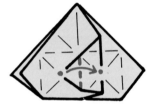

12 Notice the two small boxes that lie on the bottom edge of your paper; each has an **X** in the center. Bring the far right corner (front layer only) past the nearest **X** to the center of the second **X**.

13 Bring the same corner back to touch the folded edge you created in step 12.

14 In step 13, you created a triangular flap. Look for the smaller triangular flap that lies along the lower edge of this one. Fold the smaller triangular flap upward. Crease firmly and unfold.

15 Put your finger inside the pocket formed by the double edge at the lower edge of the large triangular flap. Remove your finger, squeeze the pocket open, and insert the smaller triangular flap into this pocket.

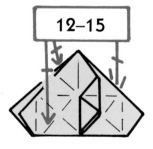

16 Repeat steps 12 through 15 on the left side of your model. Then turn your paper over and repeat on the back.

17 Slightly separate the top and bottom layers of paper and blow into the opening to inflate the ball.

18 Within each diamond shape on your ball, find the valley fold and gently press inward with a finger to give the ball a faceted look.

Action Toy: Place the model on the table so that the opening is at the top. Release the ball and it will roll over for you.

Hanging Decoration: See page 105 for instructions on hanging origami models.

GYROSCOPE

Design by Lewis Simon (Anaheim, California, USA)

PAPER:

Twelve squares of equal size. Approximately 3″ (7.5cm) square is a good size. Foil paper works well because the slippery quality of its foil side helps the units slide together at the end. Origami paper or other lightweight paper can also be used.

Lewis Simon, a member of the West Coast Origami Guild, is known for his many modular designs, including this interesting model he calls Gyroscope. Although this model does not work like a true gyroscope, it can rotate on different axes if you change the position of your hands when spinning the finished model. Mathematically, the shape created forms the skeleton of an octahedron with a cube-shaped opening in the center.

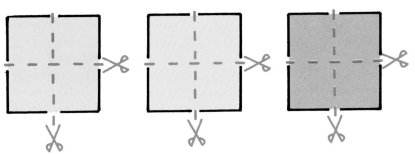

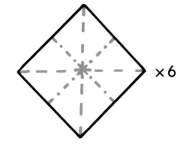

1 If you do not have twelve small squares, use three 6″ (15cm) squares and cut each into quarters.

2 Fold six of your squares into preliminary bases (see page 17). Fold the other six into waterbomb bases (see page 18).

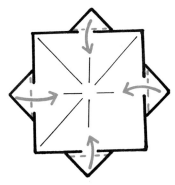

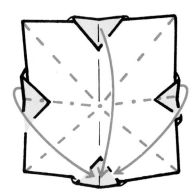

3 Half-open one preliminary base and one waterbomb base and lay them on the table, white sides facing up. Place the waterbomb base over the preliminary base so that their mountain and valley creases match each other.

4 Find the corners of the preliminary base (the lower layer) that extend out beyond the edges of the waterbomb base. Turn these corners over the edges of the waterbomb base, forming little colored triangles. Make your fold a thick hair's width away from the raw edge of the paper. This slight gap will help you later when you join the units together.

5 Reclose the preliminary and waterbomb bases and you have completed one unit.

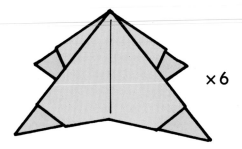

×6

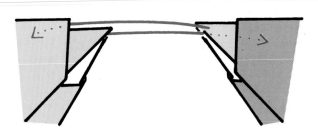

6 Repeat steps 3 through 5 with the remaining preliminary and waterbomb bases to give you a total of six completed units.

7 Assembly: Each unit has four small triangular-shaped tabs protruding out at the ends. Slightly separate the raw edges of a tab from one unit and fit it over the mountain-folded edge of a tab from a second unit. Slide the units together so that the two tabs are completely hidden.

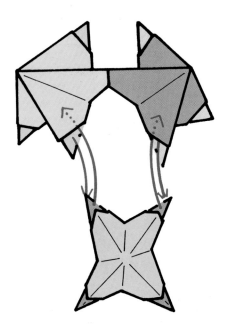

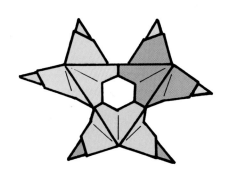

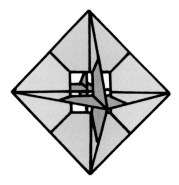

8 Take a third unit and join two of its tabs to a free tab on each of the first two units.

9 Notice the triangular outline you have created by joining the three units. Keep adding more units in a similar manner to complete the structure of your Gyroscope. Don't get discouraged with your last unit; in modulars, these are always the hardest to add.

10 Use your completed Gyroscope as a decoration, or hold it between two open palms and blow!

MAGIC STAR

Design by Robert Neale (Leeds, Massachusetts, USA)

This amazing model transforms from a ring into a star and back again. It can be used as a coaster, a napkin ring, a card or package decoration, or hanging decoration; as a ring it can be thrown like a Frisbee. For a successful model, it is very important that you fold very neatly. If the units are not folded accurately or are joined together in a sloppy manner, you will hinder the smooth sliding action of the finished model. The Magic Star is a good example of how its creator, Robert Neale, combines his interests in origami and magic.

YOU SHOULD KNOW:

Inside reverse fold

PAPER:

Eight squares of equal size, each approximately 3″ (7.5cm) square. Foil paper, origami paper, or a similar lightweight paper will all work well.

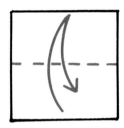

1 BOOK FOLD and UN-FOLD: Begin with one square, white side facing up. Fold your square in half and unfold.

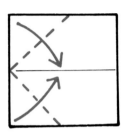

2 HOUSE-ROOF FOLD: Fold the top and bottom left corners inward to meet at the horizontal centerline. Your paper will resemble a sideways house.

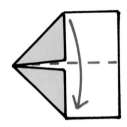

3 Fold in half along the existing horizontal crease.

This modular design is made from eight identical units linked together with a folded lock. To vary the look of your finished model, try experimenting with different color patterns:

8 different colors (1 square of each color)

4 different colors (2 squares of each color)

2 different colors (4 squares of each color)

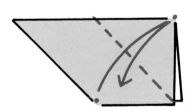

4 Fold the top right corner down so that the side raw edges lie on the bottom raw edges. Make a very sharp crease and unfold. Press your finger over the crease you just made to flatten it.

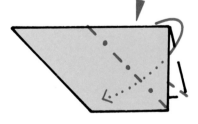

5 INSIDE REVERSE FOLD: Slightly separate the front and back layers. Push down on the right side of the top folded edge, inserting this edge in between the front and back layers. The creases you made in step 4 will now become folded edges.

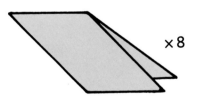

×8

6 Flatten the paper and you have your finished unit. Notice the two "arms" you have formed on the right. Repeat steps 1 through 5 with the remaining squares to give you a total of eight units.

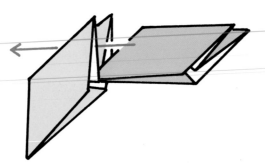

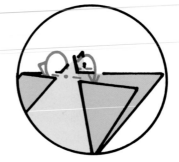

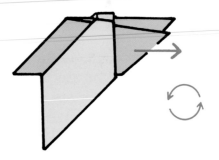

7 Study the drawing carefully and hold two units as shown: The arms of the first unit are pointing up; the arms of the second unit are at the right. Slide the second unit between the arms of the first. The second unit should sit flush against the inner groove of the first unit.

8 Wrap the protruding tips of unit one around the arms of unit two to lock the units together. Be careful to make these folds very neat but not too tight or your finished model will buckle.

9 Slide the second unit as far to the right as the lock will allow and check to make sure you have a smooth sliding action. Then rotate your model slightly so the open arms of the second unit are now pointing up.

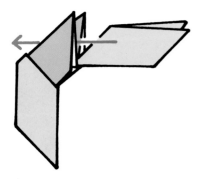

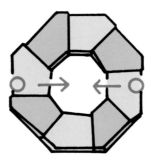

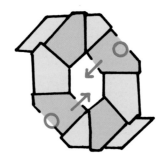

10 Hold the third unit with the arms at the right and slide it between the arms of the second unit. Make sure it sits flush against the inner groove of unit two.

11 Lock them together as you did the first two units and then slide the third unit to the right. Continue adding units until all eight are joined together. The last unit will join with the first to form a full circle.

12 The completed ring.
To transform your ring into a star: Hold the ring at opposite sides and gently push your hands together as far as the ring will comfortably allow.

Rotate the model slightly and again push your hands gently together. Continue in this manner until the star pattern is formed.

To transform back to a ring:
Hold on to the inner pattern at opposite sides of your star and pull gently apart until you are stopped by the lock in the paper. Rotate the model slightly and pull from this new position. Continue repositioning your fingers and pulling until you have a ring again.

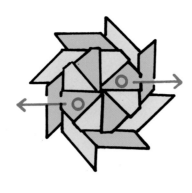

To send a greeting:
Write a greeting on the points of the star. When you open the model out to a ring, the message will disappear. When you give someone the ring, show them how to transform it into a star and the message will reappear.

KALEIDOSCOPE FLOWER

Collected by Fumio Inoue (Tokyo, Japan) and Hisa Amimoto (Chicago, Illinois, USA)

With a slight push, this flower continues to bloom over and over again! This type of rotating model is sometimes called a flexagon. The Kaleidoscope Flower is an example of modular or unit origami. Several identical units are folded separately and joined without glue to form the finished model.

★ ★ ★

PAPER:

Seven squares, each approximately 4″ (10cm) square, preferably in several different colors. Use origami paper, foil paper, gift wrap, or duo paper (a different color on each side).

To Make the Spring Unit:

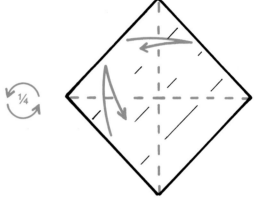

1 Begin with a square, colored side up. BOOK FOLD and UNFOLD: Bring the bottom edge up to the top edge. Crease and unfold.

2 CUPBOARD FOLD and UNFOLD: Bring the top and bottom edges inward to meet at the centerline, crease, and unfold.

3 Turn your paper over to the white side and position it so that one corner is near you. DIAPER FOLD and UNFOLD (two times): Fold and unfold your paper along each diagonal.

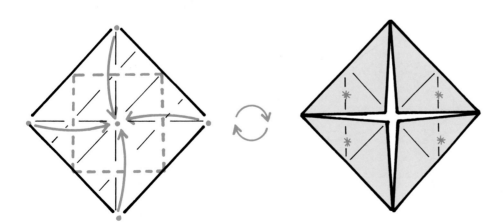

4 BLINTZ FOLD: Bring each outside corner inward to meet at the center point of your square.

5 Position the paper as shown (notice the short vertical creases [marked with an asterisk] at the sides).

6 Pick your paper up in the air. As you pinch the side corners in half with a mountain fold . . .

41

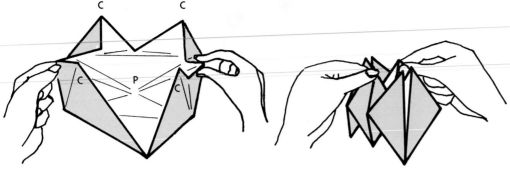

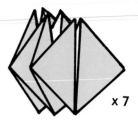

x 7

7 . . . let corners C pop up at you as center point P on the underneath layer pops down. (Note: You are not making any new creases but using the existing creases to collapse the model into the shape shown in the following drawings.)

8 Side view of move in progress.

9 Finished spring unit. Use your six remaining squares to make a total of seven identical units. Flatten each unit to sharpen the creases.

Joining the Spring Units:

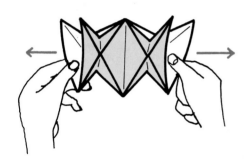

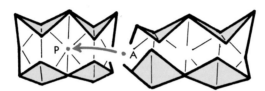

10 Insert your thumbs into the bottom of the slits on the front and back of one unit. Then pull your hands out to the sides, which will spread the unit into a half-open position as shown in the next drawing. Repeat with all seven units.

11 Make sure you see vertical creases in each unit. Find the centerpoint of the first unit. Lay the second unit over the right half of the first so that side point A touches center point P.

12 Continue joining all seven units in a like manner, always laying the new unit over the right half of the previous unit.

13 When all seven units are loosely joined, neatly reclose the units, making sure all valley and mountain folds are aligned. Squeeze the entire length of joined units together as if you were squeezing an accordion.

Assembling the Kaleidoscope Flower:

14 Release your chain of linked units. Slightly open the last unit on the right, then bend the entire chain into a circle, bringing the end units toward each other.

15 Carefully fit the left unit into the half-opened right unit so that the side point of the left unit lies over the center point of the right unit. When the two units are aligned, reclose them together to complete the ring. This is a difficult step, so have patience and keep trying.

Rotating the Kaleidoscope Flower:

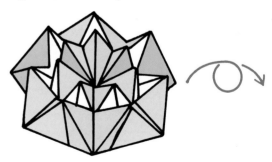

16 This view shows the bottom of your completed Kaleidoscope Flower. Turn it over . . .

 **17** ...and gently push the outer edges of the ring backward.

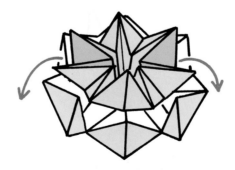 **18** Continue pushing until the ring turns completely inside out...

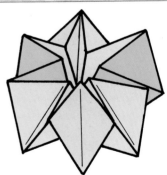 **19** ...and you are back to where you started.

Note: If any of the units come apart as you are rotating the ring, you may want to use a drop of glue to hold them together.

POP-UP SNAKE

Design by Gay Merrill Gross (New York, New York, USA)

This model is based on the Magic Flower and utilizes the same spring unit to give it its wonderful surprise action.

★★

YOU SHOULD KNOW:

Squash fold

PAPER:

Sixteen small squares, each approximately 3″ (7.5cm) square. Use origami paper, gift wrap, or bond paper. Avoid foil paper since this does not spring well. For a colorful snake, use several different-colored squares.

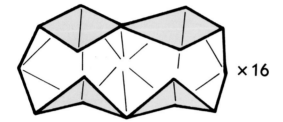

× 16

1 Follow steps 1 through 10 of the Kaleidoscope Flower on all of your small squares (you will have sixteen half-opened spring units).

2 Pick out one unit to be the head of the snake and one unit to be the tail end. Close up and flatten the head unit and position it so that the loose points are at the top.

To Form the Head:

3 On the head unit, working with the front layer only, separate the two raw edges and bring the bottom point upward to the top. Your unit will now look like . . .

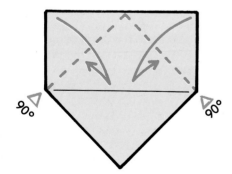

4 . . . an upside-down house. Fold the top corners down to the center. Let the flaps you just folded down partially unfold so that they are sticking straight up from the rest of the model.

5 SQUASH FOLD: On each flap that is standing up, press down on the folded edge and squash it flat to the shape of an ice cream cone. Make sure the center crease of each "cone" aligns with the split in the "ice cream."

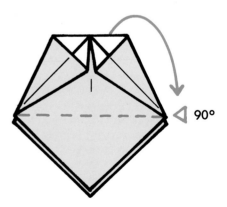

6 Bring the front flap (with the two ice cream cones) slightly forward so that it protrudes at a right angle to the rest of the layers.

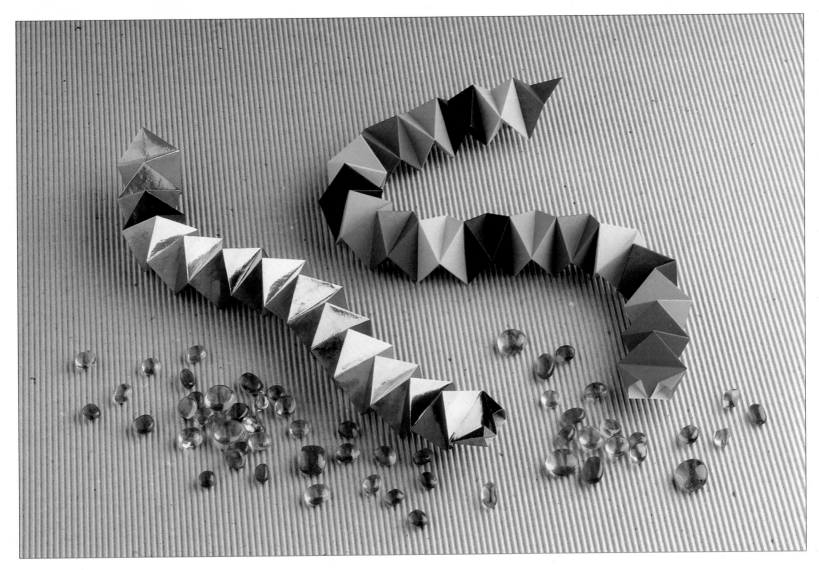

To Form the Tail:

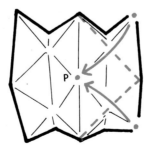

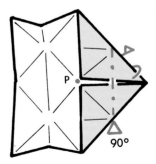

7 Slightly squeeze each "cone" to open it out. These will form two eyes, suggesting the snake's head. This is the completed head unit. It will be spread half-open when joining all the units, and it will be the first unit on the left.

8 Take the unit you have chosen to be the tail and leave it spread half-open. Find the center point of the square (P). Fold the two right corners in to meet at the center point.

9 You have formed a large colored triangle on the right half of your unit. Mountain-fold the right side point backward so that it touches the underside of center point P. Make a sharp crease and then partially unfold the same fold so that the point sticks out at the right again. This is the completed tail unit.

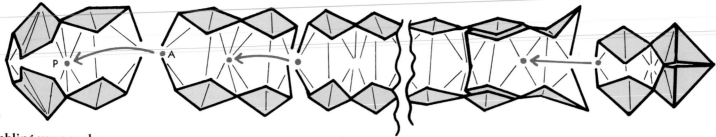

Assembling your snake:

10 Line up all sixteen of your half-opened units. Orient them as shown with the vertical creases going from top to bottom. Put the head end at the left and the tail end at the right.

11 Find the center point P of the head unit. Lay the next unit over the right half of the head unit so that side point A touches center point P.

12 Continue linking all the units in a like manner, always covering the right half of the last unit with the left half of the next unit. Make sure all valley and mountain folds are aligned.

13 Finally, join the tail-end unit to the others.

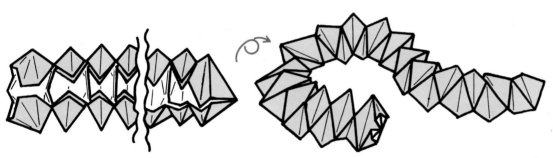

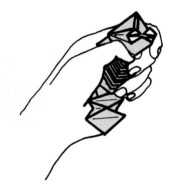

14 Now reclose all of the units, being careful not to disturb the overlapping pattern of the units. Push all of the units together as if you were squeezing an accordion. The open end is the underside of the snake. Turn it around to expose the top side.

15 Reshape the head and tail if necessary. Your finished snake can be bent into various shapes.

To have some fun:
Place the front end of the snake in your left hand, and squeeze all of the units together so that the entire model fits in your left hand, with only the head and tail sticking out.

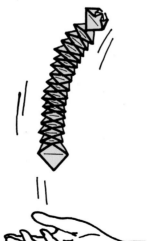

Here are some other ideas you can try with your Pop-Up Snake:

• Squeeze your snake up as tightly as it will go, and carefully place it inside a small box with a lid. When the lid is opened, the snake will pop out at unsuspecting friends.

• Make a snake from about eight units. Glue or tape the tail end of your snake to the inside of a greeting card and then compress it before closing the card and enclosing it in an envelope. This makes a fun pop-up greeting.

• Increase the number of units you fold and make a superlong snake.

Introduce your pet snake to a friend and then quickly open your left hand, causing the snake to jump out of your hand.

JACK-IN-THE-BOX

This action toy incorporates several models from this book. Jack's head and arms come from a model called Jumping Jack designed by Nick Robinson of Sheffield, England.

YOU SHOULD KNOW:

Waterbomb base
Inside reverse fold
Squash fold

PAPER:

Jack's head and arms—one square, 4⅛″ (10.6cm)
Jack's "spring" body—five squares, 3″ (7.5cm)
Box—one square, 8½″ (21.5cm)
Lid—one square, 6″ (15cm)

If you want to make a larger or smaller model, determine the size of paper for Jack as follows:

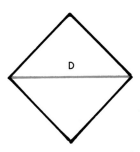

Square used for body

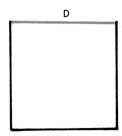

Square used for head and arms

Diagonal of body squares
(D) = length of side of head/arms square

To Make Jack's Head and Arms:

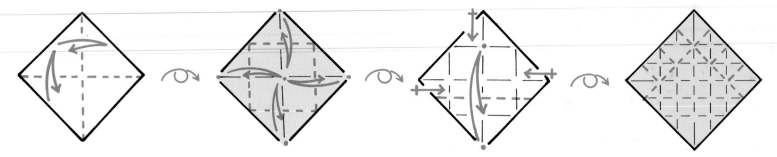

1 DIAPER FOLD and UN-FOLD (two times): With the white side facing up, fold and unfold along both diagonals. Turn over to the colored side.

2 BLINTZ FOLD and UN-FOLD: Bring each outside corner to the center point. Crease and unfold. Turn over to the white side.

3 Match the dots: Bring the bottom corner up to the far-thest crease. Crease and unfold. Rotate paper and repeat step on the other corners.

4 Turn the model back to the colored side. Make the creases shown in the drawing.

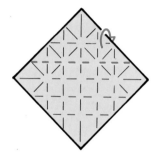

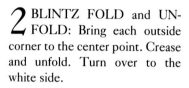

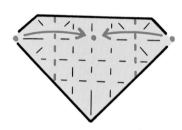

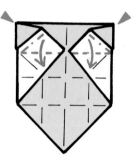

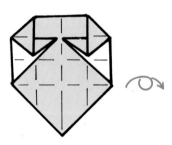

5 Mountain-fold backward on the existing crease above the horizontal centerline.

6 On the existing creases, fold the right and left side corners to the vertical centerline.

7 Push down at the top cor-ners, squashing down along the creases shown to give you the form of drawing 8.

8 Notice the two sharp points that meet at the vertical cen-terline. These arms will flip out to the sides in the next step. Turn your model over.

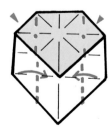

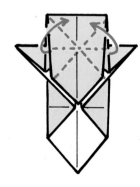

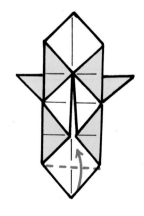

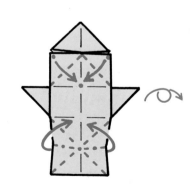

9 Press inward at the small col-ored edges. As you inside-reverse-fold along the creases shown, allow the arms from the back to swing out to the sides (see the next drawing).

10 On the front layer: Folding along the existing water-bomb-base creases, push in at the sides of the horizontal crease and swing the loose point up to the top.

11 Fold up the bottom tip of the model. Turn the model over.

12 At the bottom: Make the diagonal creases shown, then collapse the model into a waterbomb base.
At the top: Fold the corners down as for a house-roof fold.

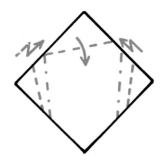

13 Turn back to the front of the model. Make a valley fold at Jack's waist. Crease and unfold halfway. The next drawings show the head only.

14 Head: Fold the top corner down to form hair; pleat the side corners to form ears.

15 Mountain-fold the top corners to give the head a rounder shape.

16 Pull down slightly on the loose bottom point but retain the waterbomb base shape below the waist. Jack's head and arms are finished and ready to be joined to the body.

To Make Jack's Body:

1 Make and join five spring units by following steps 1 through 13 of the Kaleidoscope Flower.

2 Open out the end of unit one and slip its top edge under Jack's arms. Align Jack and the body so that all mountain and valley folds match.

3 Reclose the units so that Jack is securely joined to the body and standing up.

To Make the Box:
Fold the square into a cube-shaped box as described on page 60 (instructions for box variations, making a deeper box).

To Make the Lid:
Fold the square into a *masu* box according to the instructions on page 55.

Assembly:
Glue or tape the bottom of Jack's spring body to the bottom of the cube box. Compress Jack's body and push him down into the box. As you hold Jack down with one finger, cover the box with the lid. Coach Jack out of the box by humming the tune to "Pop Goes the Weasel." When you get to the "Pop!" part of the song, remove the lid and watch Jack jump out!

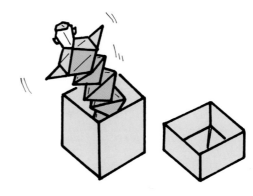

BUTTERFLY BALL

Design by Kenneth Kawamura (East Lansing, Michigan, USA)

YOU SHOULD KNOW:

Waterbomb base

PAPER:

Twelve squares, each approximately 2¾" (7cm) square. Lightweight paper such as origami paper is not sturdy enough for this model. Choose paper of a heavier weight (around twenty-four-pound), such as good-quality stationery or neon bond. Ideally, you would like the units to be white or all the same color on the outside and multicolored on the inside. If your paper is too lightweight or the same color on both sides, you can glue two sheets of paper together or color one side of your paper.

This delightful model is something you will want to show off to friends. The seemingly solid geometric shape explodes into a cascade of colorful butterflies when hit openhanded in midair! The units of this model are very simple to make, but assembling it can be very frustrating since the model seems to want to come apart at almost every step. The secret is patience and practice. It becomes easier to assemble after you have put it together a few times and are familiar with its geometric pattern.

Kenneth Kawamura's fascination with geometry is evident in this model and in his numerous other designs, which include wonderful containers and a series of more than fifty dollar-bill rings.

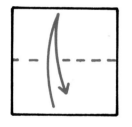

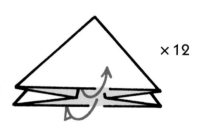

1 The side that is facing up now will be the outside or "container" side, which may be white or a plain solid color. BOOK FOLD and UNFOLD: Fold the paper in half and unfold.

2 Turn your paper over to the other side so the pretty or "butterfly" side is facing up. DIAPER FOLD and UNFOLD (two times): Fold the paper diagonally in half in both directions.

3 Collapse the paper into a waterbomb-base shape. (Unlike a regular waterbomb base, this unit has only one book fold in it.) This completes one unit, which should be plain on the outside and pretty on the inside.

4 Repeat steps 1 through 3 on the remaining squares to give you twelve units. Sharpen your creases, then half-open each unit so that it appears as in the next drawing. If your units are too closed or too open, it will make assembly more difficult.

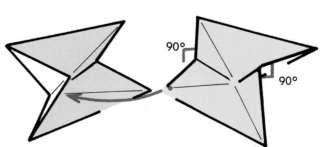

5 Orient the first four units so that they sit on a flat triangular face.

6 Lay one unit on a table so that one triangular face rests on the table. Lay a bottom point of a second unit inside a bottom point of the first. (Note: Some people prefer to assemble this model in their hand.)

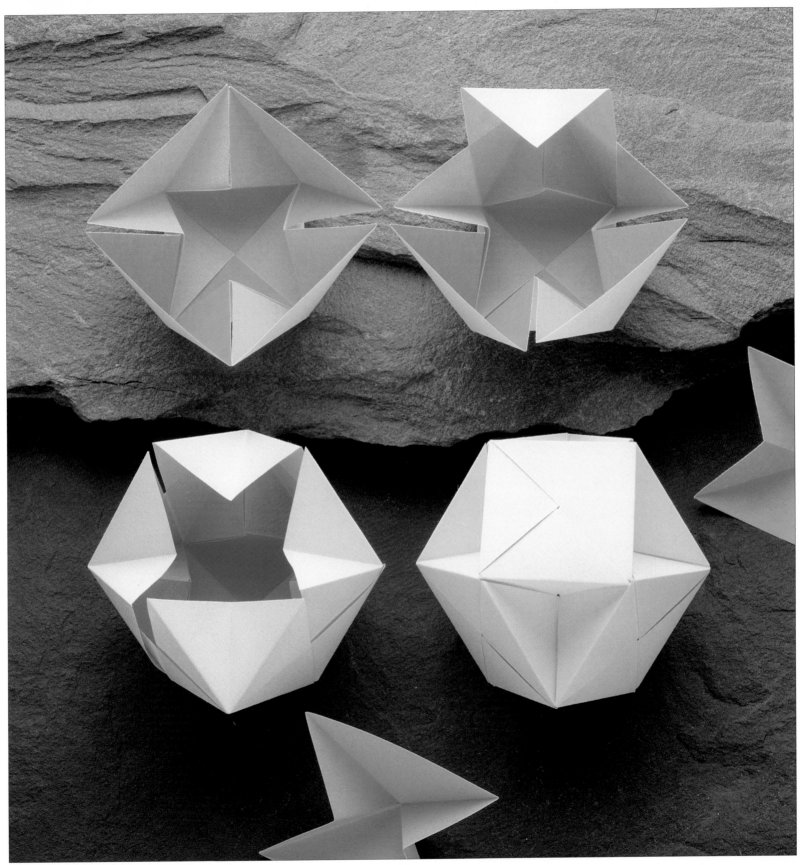

7 In a similar manner, lay a bottom point of a third unit inside the free bottom point of the second.

8 Lay a fourth unit inside the third and outside the first. Slide units together as far as they will go.

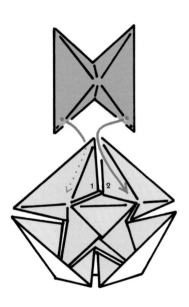

9 This completes the bottom face of the geometric form. Notice the square shape created at the bottom of the interlocking units. This square face, or "four-unit weave" will be repeated six times on the final form.

10 For this next tier of four units added, take four new units and turn them sideways so that the straight sides are at the right and left and the bent sides are at the top and bottom.

11 Look at the already assembled units and locate a place where two bent sides of two adjacent units meet. Determine which unit lies over the other. The one on top is unit two and the other is unit one. Take a new unit and insert one of its bottom points inside unit two and the other outside unit one. When pushed together, these three units will form the shape of a triangular pyramid that inverts into the model.

A Great Hint comes from Thoki Yenn of Copenhagen, Denmark. To aid in assembling the Butterfly Ball, place the interwoven, four bottom units inside a shallow box (see box variations on page 59), and then continue adding units. The bottom of the box should be slightly larger than the square you used for each unit. The height of the box should be approximately one inch (2.5cm).

A cube-shaped box, with the shallow box as a lid, can be used to transport the assembled ball.

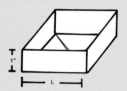

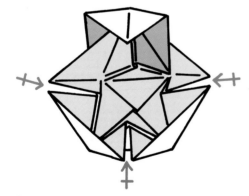

12 It is at this point that your model will begin to fall apart. Push the units back together. Repeat step 11 three more times with three new units being added to the loose corners of the assembled base. Some folders have found masking tape or other removable tape or a small container (such as the shallow box on page 59) helpful in holding the units together until they are more familiar with assembling the model. If you resort to tape, make sure you remove it before you explode the model at the end.

13 If your units are separating, slide them back together to give you the shape shown in the drawing. Notice that in between each inverted pyramid, three units overlap to form a flat square-shaped surface. You will be adding a fourth unit to each of these faces to make it a "four-unit weave."

Orient the last four units so that a flat triangular face is facing up and the bent sides are at the right and left. The bottom points of a free unit are inserted over one loose point of the assembled form and under the neighboring point. Remember the rule: Always insert a point into a unit that is covered by another and over a unit that is already covering another.

14 Your next free unit will be inserted over and under three loose points on the assembled form. It will complete another "four-unit weave" and create another inverted triangular pyramid. Remember the over-and-under rule. Repeat this step with the second-to-last unit.

15 Your last unit will be inserted under and over four loose points. This is the most difficult unit to add so have patience. The last unit also completes your sixth "four-unit weave" at the very top surface of the model.

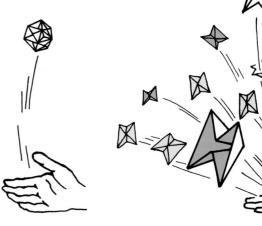

16 Gently go around the shape and make sure all your units are slid together as far as possible. The resulting shape is called a cuboctahedron. After all this work you may be reluctant to burst the model open, but you will find the model easier to put together after you have practiced a few times.

17 To burst the model: Throw it gently up in the air. As it begins to descend, punch the ball straight up again with an open hand, giving it a good strong smack. The model will burst open with a spray of color and then shower down to the ground.

Butterfly Ball Story

Add interest and drama to your demonstration of the Butterfly Ball by introducing it with a short story such as this one by Rachel Katz.

This ball has a very interesting story to it.
Show ball.
It's very tricky to put together, and the last time I made it, something amazing happened. I was outdoors on a very windy day. I was almost finished making the ball when I saw some beautiful butterflies fly by. Then the wind blew away one of my papers, and I ran to chase after it. When I came back, I finished putting the ball together. But then I noticed that the butterflies were gone, and strangely enough, I thought I heard a soft noise from inside the ball. Here, listen.
Hold the ball up to the ear of someone in the audience and secretly tap or wiggle the ball to give the impression of butterflies fluttering inside. Let a few people in your audience "hear" the butterflies.
Do you hear the noise? I think the butterflies flew into my ball and are trapped inside. If there are butterflies in here, I think they would be

much happier if we let them out. Do you think we should set them free? Okay, I'll set them free on the count of three. One, two . . .
Gently throw the ball up into the air.
. . . three!
As the ball begins to descend, hit it upward again by smacking it hard with your hand, palm open and facing up. If done correctly, the ball will break apart and the individual units will come fluttering down, looking like butterflies.

More Butterfly Ball ideas:

• Instead of a ball of butterflies, coordinate your paper to give the impression of a starburst (silver foil paper on the inside of the units) or fireworks (an assortment of bright colors on the inside of the units).

• The Butterfly Ball can also be used like a piñata at a party. Remove one unit and fill the ball with very small origami models, very lightweight favors, or clues to a treasure hunt, then replace the unit. When the ball is burst open, party guests can scurry to pick up the contents.

Boxes, Bags, and Other Containers

MASU BOX

Traditional Design

★★
PAPER:

A square of origami paper, foil paper, or wrapping paper is acceptable for smaller boxes. For sturdier boxes, use heavier paper such as bond paper, marbleized paper, wallpaper, decorative shopping bags, or covers from magazines cut into squares. Each side of your finished box will be approximately one-third the length of your original square. The height of the box will be approximately one-sixth the size of the starting square.

This traditional model is called *masu* in Japan because it resembles a box used for measuring. Boxes of different sizes would serve as standard measures just as we might use measuring cups of different sizes for baking. This model offers many possibilities for experimenting with different kinds of paper. By varying the folding pattern of the box itself, boxes of many different proportions can be created.

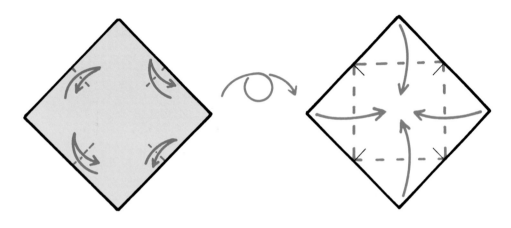

1 Begin with the colored side of the square facing up. BOOK FOLD and UNFOLD (twice): Fold and unfold the square in half in both directions. If you do not want these creases to show on your finished box, crease only near the side edges of the square and leave the middle uncreased. Each long "pinch" should be approximately one-fourth the length of one side.

2 Turn your paper over to the white side. BLINTZ FOLD: Use the creases from step 1 as a guide to fold all four corners to the center.

3 CUPBOARD FOLD and UNFOLD: Bring the top and bottom edges inward to meet at the center. Crease sharply and unfold.

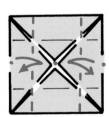

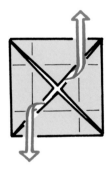

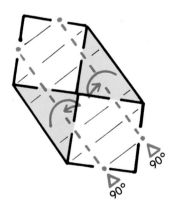

4 CUPBOARD FOLD and UNFOLD: Bring the right and left sides inward to meet at the center. Crease sharply and unfold.

5 Unfold the top and bottom triangular flaps.

6 Refold on the existing creases that connect the far dots. Crease sharply and then partially unfold so that the two flaps stand at a right angle to the rest of the model. They form two sides of your box.

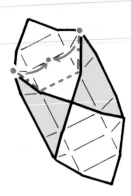

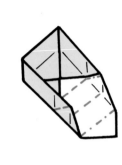

7 For this step you will be folding simultaneously on three existing creases: Push inward on the small mountain-fold creases where the color and white meet. At the same time, valley-fold on the crease that connects these two mountain folds.

8 You should now have formed the third side of your box. Grasp the long tab that sticks up and pull it down and inside the box so that it lines the inside of the box.

9 Repeat steps 7 and 8 on the other open end of your box.

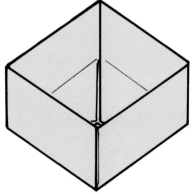

Optional Box "tricks":
• To keep the four flaps that line the inside of your box from "popping" up: Lift the flaps up for a moment and place a small piece of tape, sticky side up, in the center of the box. Replace the flaps so that they stick to the tape and also cover it so it is hidden from view.

• For an extra-sturdy box, cut a piece of cardboard to fit in the bottom. Unfold the box back to step 7 and insert the cardboard under the two bottom flaps. Then refold the box and the cardboard will be hidden.

10 Reinforce the creases on finished Box.

BOX COVER

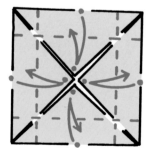

Use a square the same size as the square you used for the *masu* box. Follow the instructions for the box but replace steps 3 and 4 with the following:

3 and 4. Fold the bottom edge up to lie approximately ⅛" (0.3cm) below the center. (The size of the gap may vary from ¹/₁₆" to ³/₁₆" [0.2 to 0.4cm] depending on the thickness of the paper you are using.) Crease sharply and unfold. Repeat on all four sides of the blintzed square. Continue from step 5 of the box.

Fit the finished cover over the box.

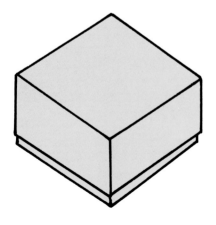

BOX DIVIDER

Design by Paolo Bascetta (Bologna, Italy)

★★
YOU SHOULD KNOW:
Waterbomb base

PAPER:
A square the same size as
the square you used for folding
the Box.

Paolo Bascetta is a member of the Italian origami group, Centro Diffusione Origami. His very clever Divider turns the traditional Japanese *masu* box (page 55) into a useful container with four separate compartments. By putting the two models together, you have a wonderful holder for small desk items or even jewelry. By turning it sideways, you can use it as a shelf display for miniature origami models.

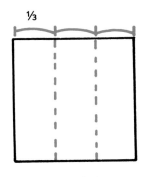

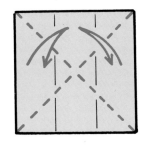

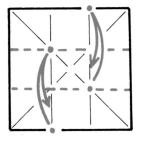

1 With the white side facing up, fold your square into thirds, then turn it over to the colored side.

2 DIAPER FOLD and UNFOLD (twice): Fold your paper in half along both diagonals, then turn it back to the white side and position your paper so that the creases made in step 1 are vertical.

3 Divide the model into thirds: Bring the bottom edge to the farthest intersection of creases (match dot to dot). Crease and unfold. Repeat with the top edge.

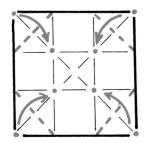
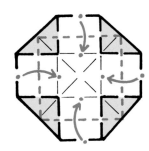
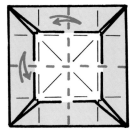

4 Fold each outside corner to the nearest intersection of creases.

5 Fold each raw edge to the nearest crease.

6 BOOK FOLD and UNFOLD (twice): Fold the model in half in both directions. Then turn the model over.

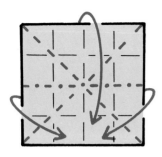

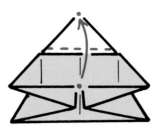

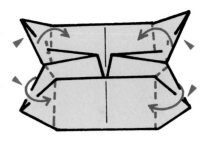

7 Using the existing creases, collapse your paper into a waterbomb base.

8 Lift the bottom edge (of the front layer only) to the top point of the model. This will form the three-dimensional shape shown in the next drawing.

9 Gently push the outside points inward to form the model into the two rectangular box shapes shown in the next drawing.

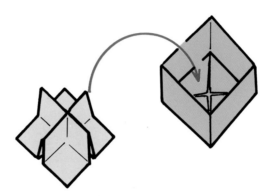

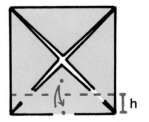

10 Mountain-fold the model in half down the vertical centerline. The result is . . .

11 . . . a plus-sign standing on top of four little squares. This is your finished Box Divider.

12 Insert the Divider into the Box. Add a cover if you wish.

BOX VARIATIONS

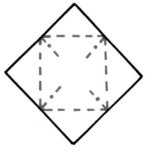

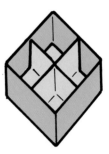

MAKING A DEEP OR SHALLOW BOX

You can vary the height of your box by varying the amount you fold the sides inward after the paper is folded into a blintz fold.

1 Follow steps 1 and 2 for the *masu* box.

2 **To make a shallower box:** Fold the bottom edge up to a spot below the center. (Distance h equals the height of your finished box.) Crease sharply and unfold. Rotate your paper one-quarter turn.

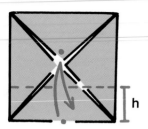

To make a deeper box: Fold the bottom edge past the center (but not more than one-third the length of the present size of your paper). Crease sharply and unfold. Rotate your paper one-quarter turn.

3 Using intersection point A as a guide, fold the bottom edge up an equal amount as in step 2. Crease sharply and unfold.

4 Repeat step 3 on the remaining two sides of your square.

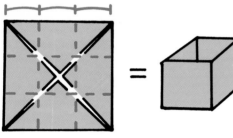

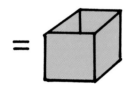

Note: If you fold your paper in thirds in steps 2 through 4, your finished box will be the shape of a cube.

5 Continue from step 5 of the *masu* box.

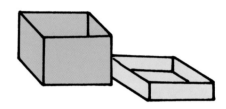

Your completed shallow and deep boxes will look similar to these. Experiment with different-size papers to see if you can make a shallow box to fit as a lid on a deep box.

RECTANGULAR BOX

All of the box variations we have made thus far have all had square bottoms. Here's how to vary the same box so that it has a rectangular bottom.

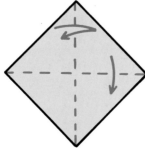

1 Begin with the colored side facing up. Diaper-fold and unfold in both directions. Leave in the second diaper fold.

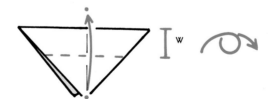

2 Fold one bottom corner up past the top edge of the paper. (Distance w will be the width of your finished box.) Turn over.

3 Make sure the vertical centerline creases are aligned. Then fold up the bottom corner to match the top corner. (If you are making a lid for your box, take a second sheet of paper and follow steps 1 through 3, making sure distance w is the same on both sheets.)

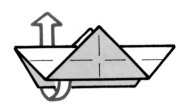

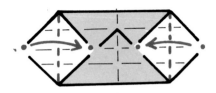

4 Bring the bottom folded edge (front layer only) up to the long folded edge. Crease sharply and unfold. Turn the paper over and repeat. (For a box lid: Bring the bottom folded edge up to slightly below the long folded edge.)

5 Unfold the horizontal mountain fold. The two top points will cross each other on the flattened paper.

6 Fold the right and left side corners inward to the nearest intersection of raw edges and you will completely cover the white.

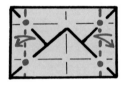

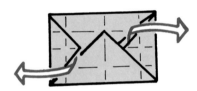

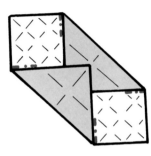

7 Connect the dots: Fold the right and left side edges inward, making a valley fold that connects the points marked (the intersection of the raw edges and the crease). Crease sharply and unfold.

8 Unfold the triangular flaps back out to the sides.

9 Pinch mountain folds where shown in the drawing.

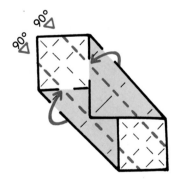

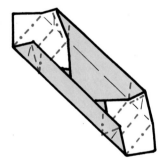

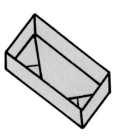

10 Fold the long sides up to stand at a right angle to the rest of the paper. This will form two sides of your box.

11 Form the last two sides in the same manner as for the *masu* box.

12 Completed Rectangular Box.

CARD CASE

Design by Humiaki Huzita (Padua, Italy)

This very simple design makes a useful case for small cards such as business cards, credit cards, identification cards, or membership cards. Children can use the case to hold a library card or a bus pass. The creator of this model is a professor of physics who was born in Japan but now teaches at the University of Padua in Italy.

PAPER:

Use a sheet of A4 or letter-size paper (8½″ × 11″ [21.5 × 28cm]).

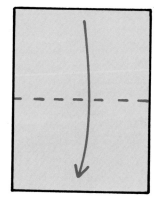

1 If your paper has a color or pattern on only one side, begin with that side facing up. Bring the short top edge down to meet the short bottom edge, folding the paper in half.

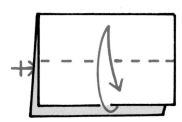

2 Bring the bottom raw edge (front layer only) up to the top folded edge. Crease and unfold. Turn over and repeat on the other side.

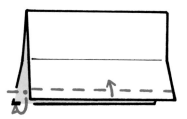

3 On the front layer, fold the bottom raw edge up approximately ½″ (1.5cm) to create a small hem. Then turn your model to the back and fold up a matching hem on the back layer.

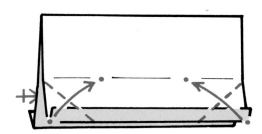

4 On the front layer, fold the bottom corners up to the horizontal crease. Turn the model over and repeat.

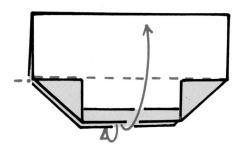

5 On the front layer, refold on the existing horizontal crease. Repeat on the other side.

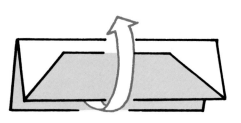

6 Unfold the top folded edge.

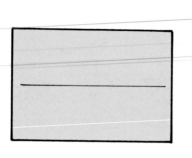

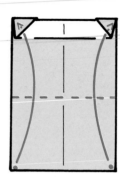

7 Rotate your paper one-quarter turn, so the short edges are at the top and bottom.

8 Fold down the top edge to form a hem approximately 1″ (2.5cm) wide.

9 Notice the two triangular pockets at either side of the hem. Bring the bottom edge upward and insert its corners into the triangular pockets. Slide the bottom edge as far up as it will comfortably fit inside the pockets and then make a firm crease along the new bottom edge.

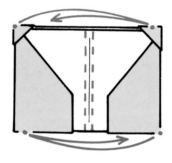

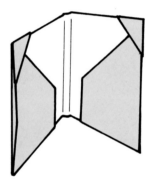

10 Fold the left side of the model over to almost touch the right side, leaving a small gap. Crease firmly, then unfold. Repeat, bringing the right side almost to the left. These two folds form the spine of your case.

11 Your case is now complete. You will find four pockets for holding cards, two on the outside and two on the inside.

CARD CASE VARIATIONS

PICTURE FRAME CASE

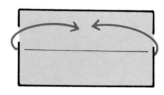

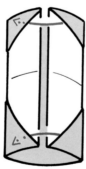

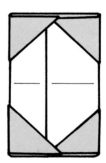

1 Follow steps 1 through 6 of the Card Case. Bend the short sides of the model toward each other.

2 Slip the corners of one end into the pockets of the other end. Slide the two ends together until the model is a little wider than the size of the card or other item you wish it to hold. Press down firmly on the folded sides.

3 Form a spine for the case as you did in step 10 of the original Card Case. Or leave the model flat without a spine and use it as a picture frame.

PORTFOLIO

You can fold either the Card Case or Picture Frame Case design from larger paper to use as a portfolio for holding larger items. Suggested folding papers include marbleized paper, a poster, a map, fadeless paper, or kraft paper.

• To make a case to hold 6″ (15cm) origami paper: Start with a sheet 16″ × 27″ (41 × 69cm).

• To make a portfolio for letter-size paper: Use a sheet 28″ × 40″ (70 × 100cm).

CARD OR PHOTO HOLDER

Design by Ralph Matthews (Cheshire, England)

PAPER:
Two rectangles of equal size in the proportion 2:1. A 6″ (15cm) or smaller square can be cut in half to give you two rectangles.

As a magician, Ralph Matthews frequently uses playing cards for folding. He also has found many uses for simple origami models. Here the Magic Pocket becomes a practical holder for place cards at a party or small signs at an exhibition. You also may want to make several holders and use them as corner hinges to hold photos for display.

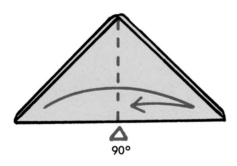

90°

1 Fold each rectangle into a Magic Pocket (see page 27). Fold each model in half. Crease sharply and partially unfold the last crease.

2 Stand the models on a table as shown and insert your card or photo into one pocket of each model.

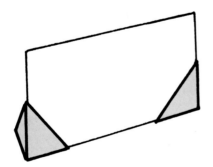

3 Here is your completed Card Holder.

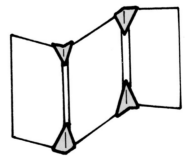

Use several small corner hinges to join photographs for display.

WALLET

Design by Nick Robinson (Sheffield, England)

Nick Robinson is involved in origami as a teacher and author as well as creator. For the British Origami Society magazine, he writes a column on origami activities around the world. This design is very useful as a wallet and can also be used as a decorative container when giving money or a check as a gift.

Letter-size paper. Credit cards and most sizes of currency will fit in a wallet folded from A4 or 8½" × 11" (21.5 × 28cm) paper. For larger-size currencies, use slightly larger paper, such as 9" × 12" (23 × 31cm). The model can be folded from bond paper, stationery, gift wrap, or a magazine cover. For an especially beautiful and strong wallet, use Japanese *washi* paper.

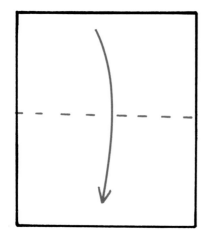

1 Begin with the white side facing up and the short sides of the rectangle at the top and bottom. Bring the top edge down to the bottom edge, folding the paper in half.

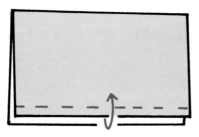

2 Lift the bottom edge of the front layer only and fold it up approximately ⅜" (0.8cm) to form a small hem.

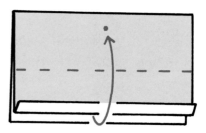

3 Bring the folded edge of the hem up to lie approximately ⅝" (1.5cm) below the top edge of the model.

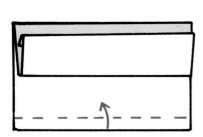

4 Fold up the bottom raw edge to form a hem approximately ½" (1.3cm) wide.

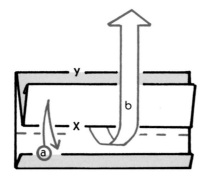

5 a) Make a valley fold at or slightly below edge X. Crease and unfold.
b) Grasp folded edge X and lift it upward, unfolding folded edge Y.

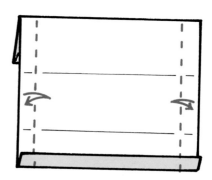

6 Fold in the right and left sides of the paper to form a hem on each side approximately ⅝" (1.5cm) wide. Crease sharply and unfold.

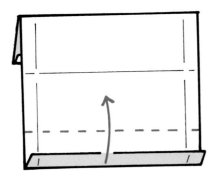

7 Refold on the valley crease nearest the bottom edge.

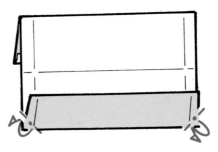

8 Mountain-fold the bottom corners up to the nearest crease. Make a sharp crease and unfold. (It is easiest to do this by turning the model over to the back and then returning it to the front position when the fold is complete.)

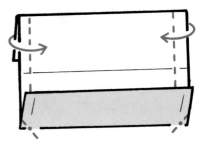

9 On all but the front layer, fold the right and left sides inward on the existing hem creases. At the same time, the small slanted folds at the bottom of the front layer should be folded backward to accommodate for the hem creases.

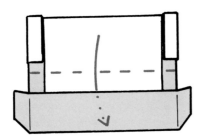

10 Folding on the existing horizontal crease, bring the top edge down and insert behind the wide band at the bottom.

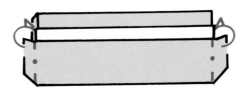

11 Mountain-fold the protruding tabs and tuck them in between the double layers at the side ends of the model.

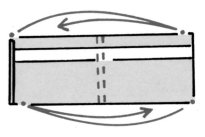

12 Fold the left side of the model over to lie just short of the right edge. Crease firmly and unfold. Repeat, bringing the right side almost to the left. This forms the Wallet's spine.

13 Completed Wallet. Optionally, you may wish to add a small bit of glue to the tabs you inserted in step 11.

SHOPPING BAG

Design by Fred Rohm (Williamsport, Pennsylvania, USA)

★★

PAPER:

A large rectangle of paper such as
gift-wrap paper, kraft paper,
or a map.

Fred Rohm, known for his very complicated and ingenious origami designs, created this model after someone showed him a shopping bag they had made with glue. Fred took up the challenge to create the same bag–but without glue. This bag makes a wonderful container for a gift or some of your loose origami models.

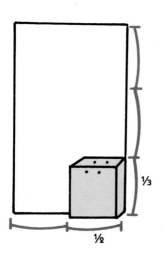

Figuring bag dimensions

The width of the finished bag will be one-half the length of the short side of the rectangle you start with.

The height of the bag will be approximately one-third the length of the long side of the rectangle.

Thus a rectangle 10″ × 16″ (26 × 40cm) will make a bag 5″ (13cm) wide and 5″ (13cm) high.

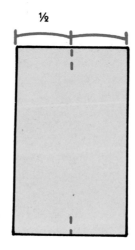

1 Begin with the colored side of the paper facing up. Make a pinch mark at the center of the short edges.

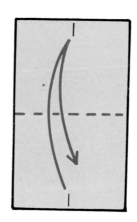

2 BOOK FOLD and UN-FOLD: Fold the paper in half, bringing the short sides together. Crease and unfold. Then turn your paper over to the white side.

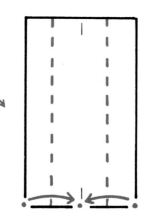

3 CUPBOARD FOLD: Bring the long sides inward to meet at the center. Use the pinch marks made in step 1 as your guide.

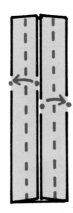

4 Fold each long raw edge back out to the folded edge.

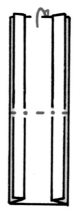

5 Mountain-fold the paper in half along the existing crease: Bring the top edge backward to lie behind the bottom edge.

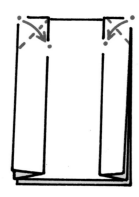

6 Fold the top corners down to the vertical folded edge, forming two small triangles.

68

7 Take the front layer only and fold it upward as far as the corner triangles will allow. Make a sharp crease and then unfold this crease and the two triangles. Turn your paper over and repeat steps 6 and 7 on the back.

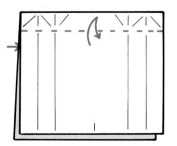

8 Completely unfold the paper, then put back the original book fold from step 2. Fold the front layer up along the existing horizontal crease. Repeat on the other side. Make sure the raw edges match at the top, then unfold both creases.

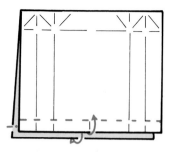
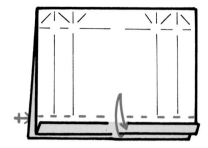
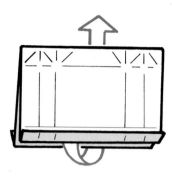

9 Fold the bottom raw edge (front layer only) up to form an even hem approximately ½″ to 1″ (1.2–2.5cm) wide. Repeat on the back, being careful to match the folded edges exactly.

10 Evenly fold the hem up one more time to make a double hem. Then turn the paper over and make a hem that exactly matches on the back. Unfold the second hems, leaving a single hem on the front and back bottom edges.

11 Unfold the center book fold but leave in the single hems. Leave your paper with the white side facing up.

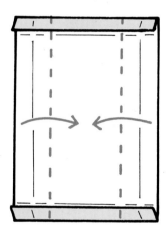
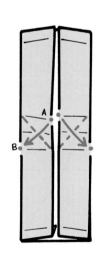
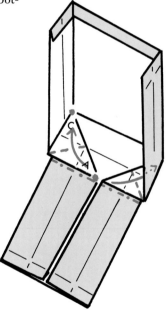

12 Refold on the cupboard folds.

13 Grasp the raw edge at point A. Bring A to B, folding along the existing diagonal crease. The top of your model will stand up at a right angle to the rest of the model as shown in the next drawing. Repeat on the right side.

14 Fold the triangle in half on the existing crease by bringing point A to point C. At the same time, the cupboard-fold flap that is flat on the table will rise up and line the inside of the flap that is standing up. Repeat on the right.

15 The cutaway view shows the inside of the bag. At the top of the bag, slip the inside layer under the hem of the outside layer to interlock them. This is done on both the right and left sides.

16 Roll the top hem down again along the existing crease to form a double hem. As you do this, hold the bag tightly where the sides overlap so that they do not slide apart.

17 Your bag is finished. Punch holes at the top hem and use a decorative cord or ribbon to make handles. Alternatively, the ends of a folded paper strip can be slipped under the hem after step 15 and locked onto the bag as the hem is rolled over a second time. The bag can be flattened for storage.

Optional: To strengthen the bag, cut a piece of cardboard to fit in the bottom.

BASKET

Design by Aldo Putignano (Clifton, New Jersey, USA)

The Basket is one of many containers and other functional origami models by Aldo Putignano. Many of his wonderful designs were created by varying the shape and folding patterns of existing models. Aldo, an art teacher, also likes to experiment by folding from interesting papers. He frequently uses paper-backed wallpaper for larger models.

★★★

PAPER:

One square for the basket, approximately 8″ (20cm) long on a side. For the handle, you will need a strip as long as the square used for the basket, or longer if you like a long-handled look. The proportion for the handle should be approximately 4:1. Alternatively, you can cut letter-size paper into a square and use the excess strip as a handle. For variety, try a ribbon handle. Use the ribbon as is, without folding it into quarters as described in the folding instructions for the paper handle.

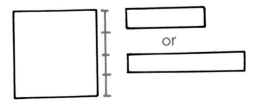

Handle:

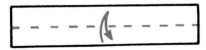

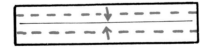

1 With the white side facing up, bring the long edges of the strip together, folding it in half. Crease and unfold.

2 Bring the long edges inward to meet at the centerline.

3 Refold the handle on the centerline.

4 Finished handle.

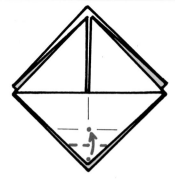

Basket:

1 Begin with a square folded into a preliminary base (see page 17). The open end should be facing away from you. Fold the top corner (front layer only) down to the bottom corner.

2 Bring the bottom, single corner up to almost touch the horizontal folded edge. Crease and unfold.

3 Bring the bottom, single corner up to the crease you made in the last step.

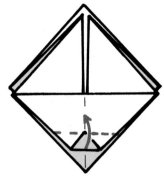

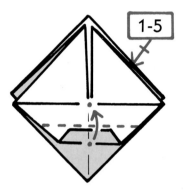

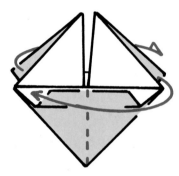

4 Refold up on the existing crease.

5 Bring the folded edge just created up to the long folded edge at the center. Then turn your model over and repeat steps 1 through 5 on the back.

6 Turn the page: Swing the near layer on the right over to the left, as if turning the page of a book. Turn the paper over and repeat.

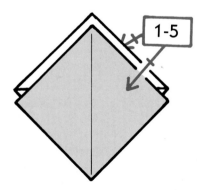

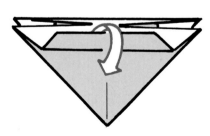

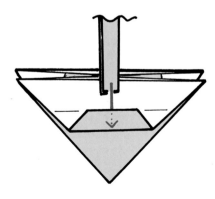

7 Your folds from the previous steps should now be hidden inside your model, and you should have a plain surface on the front and back of your model. Repeat steps 1 through 5 on these newly exposed surfaces.

8 Unfold the last fold made on the front of your model, so that it appears as in drawing 9.

9 Insert the end of the handle behind the small folded edge and slide it down as far as it will go. Make sure the handle is centered in the middle of your model.

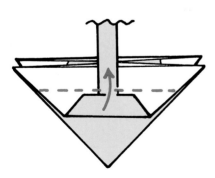

10 Refold on the existing crease, folding up the handle at the same time.

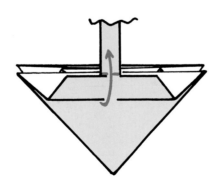

11 Bring the band at the top of your basket upward by unfolding the long folded edge at the top, to give you . . .

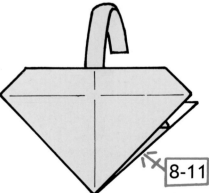

8-11

12 . . . a top shape. Turn your model over and repeat steps 8 through 11 on that side. You will need to bend the free end of your handle down to insert it into this side of the basket.

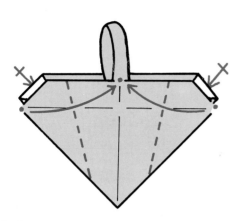

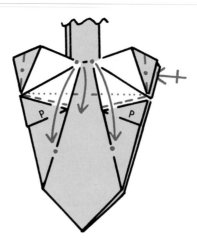

13 Match the dots: Bring the far right and left side corners (front layer only) inward to meet at the midpoint of the top folded edge of the basket. Turn the paper over and repeat.

14 In this step you will be making three separate folds at the same time and performing a modified squash. As you fold down simultaneously on the three valley folds shown, the mountain folds at the sides will be created as a result of the squash. The finished move will look like drawing 15. Repeat this step on the other side.

15 Mountain-fold the tabs that extend beyond the sides of the basket on a line that matches each basket side. Be sure to mountain-fold this layer right behind itself and not into interior layers of the model. Repeat on the other side.

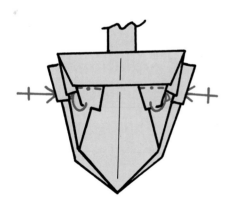

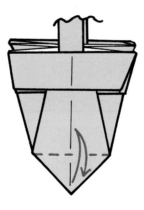

16 At the top of your basket is a band with two tabs protruding down. Lift the band and the tabs for a moment to find the folded edges marked P (for pocket) in drawing 14. Mountain-fold the tabs backward and tuck them into these triangular pockets. This will keep the band locked down in place. Turn the model over and repeat.

17 Fold the bottom point up on a line that connects the two bottom side corners and unfold.

18 Open out your model from the top of the Basket and sharpen the creases at the base of your finished Basket.

ENVELOPE

Design by Didier Boursin (Paris, France)

Didier Boursin is a former president of the French origami organization, Mouvement Français des Plieurs de Papier. His simple and elegant designs follow his philosophy of paperfolding: Create more with less paper.

This Envelope design can be used as an envelope to enclose a letter or card or as a letterfold in which the stationery you write your letter on is folded up to become its own envelope. Folded from gift wrap, this design can also be used as a lovely wrapping for a flat gift.

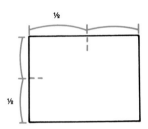

1 Pinch a long and short side of your rectangle to find the midpoint of each.

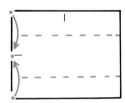

2 CUPBOARD FOLD: Fold the long sides to the center, using the pinch mark as your guide.

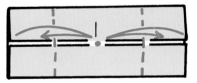

3 CUPBOARD FOLD and UNFOLD: Fold the short sides to the center, using the pinch mark as a guide. Crease firmly and unfold.

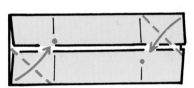

4 Fold the bottom left corner to the nearest vertical crease. Fold the top right corner to the nearest vertical crease.

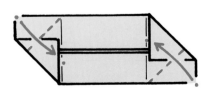

5 Fold the top left corner to the nearest crease. Fold the bottom right corner to the nearest crease.

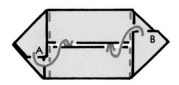

6 Notice the tabs marked A and B in the drawing. As you refold on the existing vertical creases, insert each tab into the open slit at the horizontal center of the paper. One tab will tuck downward, the other will tuck upward.

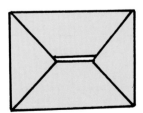

7 If you are making an envelope or letterfold, place a sticker or return-address label over the small open slit. If you are wrapping a gift, you may wish to add an origami decoration to the package.

Animals and Birds

CRANE
Traditional Design

One of the oldest paperfolds, the Crane, or *tsuru,* remains today the most popular origami model in Japan. The elegance of this design captures the grace and beauty of this bird, which is highly esteemed in Japanese culture. Their folklore says that the crane lives for a thousand years. Thus, the crane is regarded as a symbol of long life, good health, and good fortune. More recently it has come to represent the wish for peace.

Lightweight paper such as origami paper, foil paper, or gift wrap. Paper of any size can be used, but 6″ (15cm) square is recommended for your first attempts. As a challenge, some people have folded cranes from squares less than ½″ (1.3cm) in size!

This drawing is a condensation of steps 3 through 5.

1 Begin with a bird base (page 19). Make sure the split in the diamond shape is pointing toward you. Fold the lower edges (front layer only) inward to almost touch the vertical centerline. Turn the paper over and repeat.

2 The two points at the top of the model are wings. The two sharp "spikes" at the bottom will be inside-reverse-folded up and between the wings to become a neck and a tail. To simplify the inside reverse fold . . .

3 . . . turn the page: Fold the front layer at the right over to the left, as if turning the page of a book.

4 Lift the bottom point up to the top.

5 Turn the left page (front layer only) back to the right. As you do so the "spike" will be sandwiched in between the wings.

6 Before you flatten the front and back layers, pull the "spike" slightly out to the side and set it in this position by pinching the base of the wing. Repeat steps 3 through 6 on the left.

7 Inside-reverse-fold the tip of one slender point to form a head.

8 Spread the wings apart.

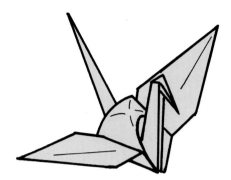

9 Hold each wing close to the central triangle. Gently pull your hands apart, causing the triangle to spread and flatten.

10 The Crane is finished. In Japanese culture, a garland of one thousand cranes represents an especially strong wish for good health. To make the garland, the cranes are usually left with their wings up (the position of the model in step 8). They are then strung on threads, one on top of the other. These same garlands are made by schoolchildren all over the world and sent to be draped across the memorial statue of Sadako Sasaki at the Hiroshima Peace Park.

CHAIN OF CRANES

One of the earliest books of origami instructions was the *Sembazuru Orikata* (*Folding a Thousand Cranes*), published in Japan in 1797. The chains of cranes in this important work are difficult to make because the cranes are all folded from the same sheet of paper, which has been slit to create many individual squares, joined only at the corners. The chain below is based on a method of interlocking the wings devised by Rhode Island folder Thomas Hull.

★ ★ ★

YOU SHOULD KNOW:

Crane

PAPER:

Two or more squares of equal size.

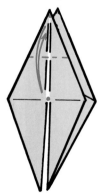

1 Begin with a bird base (see page 19). Fold one top point down to the horizontal center of the model. Crease sharply and unfold.

2 Separate the long raw edges of the diamond and again fold the top point down to the middle. Sharply crease the horizontal folded edge at the top of the triangle you have folded down. Extend this crease out to the sides.

3 Reclose the raw edges.

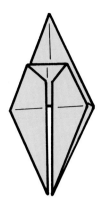

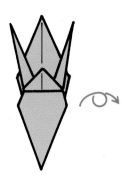

4 You have shortened one wing of your bird and created a pocket with a V-shaped opening. Leave the back wing as it is. Follow steps 1 through 6 of the Crane. Make several Cranes with one shortened wing and make one Crane in the usual manner with two full wings.

5 Fold down the full-sized wing on each bird. Then turn the models over to the side with the pocket.

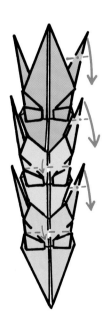

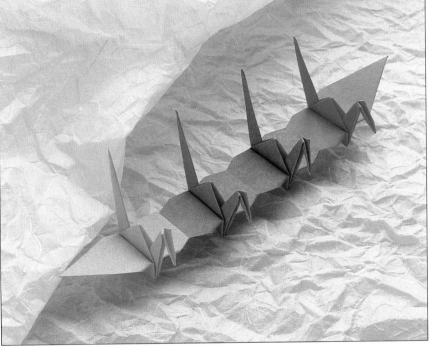

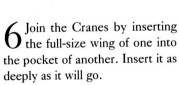

6 Join the Cranes by inserting the full-size wing of one into the pocket of another. Insert it as deeply as it will go.

7 Fold the wing with the pocket away from the body to lock the joined wings together. Inside-reverse-fold the necks to form the heads.

8 Add as many Cranes as you like to the chain. To make a lei, make a complete circle of Cranes. For extra security, you can add a drop of glue when joining the wings.

79

SPARROW

Design by Gloria Farison (Cincinnati, Ohio, USA)

This Sparrow and many other charming models have been created by Gloria Farison, an art teacher and founder of the Cincinnati Origami Guild. Her sweet-looking bird hides a secret personality. Turned upside down it becomes a Flying Vulture. (This dual feature was discovered by two Girl Scouts from Queens, New York.)

YOU SHOULD KNOW:

Rabbit ear
Bird base
Inside reverse fold

PAPER:

A square of almost any size or type of paper.

1 Begin with the white side (or the side that will end up as the bird's breast and feet) facing up. DIAPER FOLD and UNFOLD (twice): Fold the square diagonally in half in both directions.

2 RABBIT EAR: Put in the creases shown and then simultaneously fold both left sides to the vertical centerline. As you do so, the left corner will pinch in half and form an "ear" that sticks straight up.

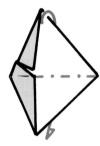

3 Mountain-fold the paper in half, bringing the top point behind to touch the bottom point.

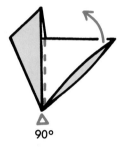
90°

4 Lift the white triangular flap straight up.

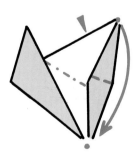

5 Squash the flap to form a small white square.

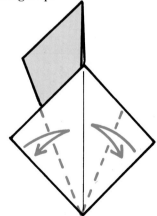

6 ICE-CREAM-CONE FOLD and UNFOLD: Fold the bottom side edges of the white square to the vertical centerline. Crease and unfold.

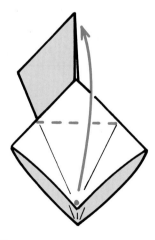

7 As you lift the front layer of the bottom corner, form a crease that connects the two creases made in the last step. The little square is opened out into a boat shape.

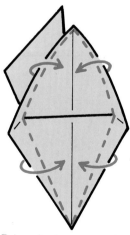

8 Bring the long raw edges together to form a tall diamond shape.

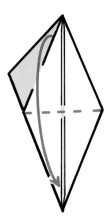 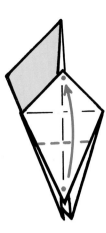 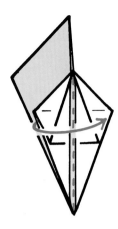 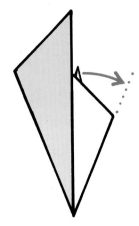

9 Fold the top point of the diamond down to the bottom to form a kite shape.

10 Fold the single bottom corner to the top of the kite.

11 Fold the left half of the kite over the right half.

12 Pull out the small tip to align with the long folded edges. (See the next drawing.)

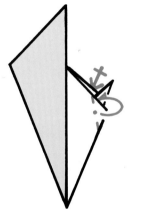 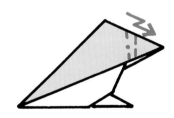 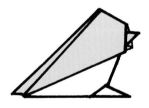

13 Mountain-fold the blunt corner of the white triangle to the interior. Repeat on the other side. Then rotate the model one quarter turn.

14 Precrease: Pleat the tip back and forth with a mountain valley fold to form the shape of the head and beak. Unfold these creases, then open out the tip and reverse-fold it in and out on the precreases to form the bird's beak.

15 The Sparrow is complete.

To form the Flying Vulture: Rotate the model so that the beak points down and becomes the tail.

The feet of the Sparrow have become the beak of the vulture. Hold the breast (under the vulture's head) in one hand. With your other hand, pull the tail back and forth to make the wings flap.

81

KOALA

Design by Yoshihide Momotani (Osaka, Japan)

Yoshihide Momotani, a professor of biology, is the author of a multitude of origami books and the patriarch of a folding family. The Momotani family frequently shows their origami work at exhibitions. One such exhibition featured scenes from fairy tales, including Hansel and Gretel's candy-covered cottage folded entirely from origami models.

A very appealing model, the Koala is also one of the most challenging in this book. Try it after you feel comfortable folding the other designs.

★★★★
YOU SHOULD KNOW:
Rabbit Ear
Squash fold
Inside reverse fold

PAPER:
A 6" (15cm) or smaller square. Origami paper or slightly heavier weight paper will work well. For a colored nose, use duo paper that is a different color on each side.

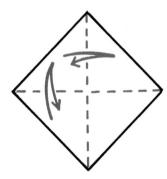

1 DIAPER FOLD and UNFOLD (twice): Begin with the white side (or nose color) of your paper facing up. Bring one corner up to meet the opposite corner. Crease and unfold. Rotate your paper and repeat this step in the other direction.

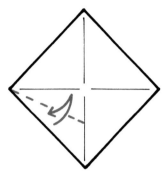

2 Bring the bottom left edge of your paper to the horizontal centerline but crease only as far as the vertical centerline.

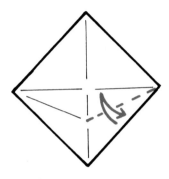

3 Repeat step 2 on the right side.

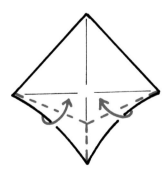

4 RABBIT EAR: Put back both creases made in steps 2 and 3 at the same time. As you do so, the bottom point will fold in half and form an "ear" that sticks up into the air.

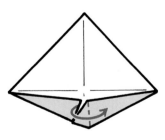

5 Fold the "ear" to the right.

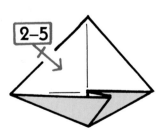

6 RABBIT EAR: Repeat steps 2 through 5 on the top half of your paper.

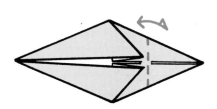

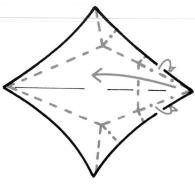

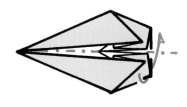

7 The resulting form is known in origami as a fish base because several traditional fish models begin with this base. Make a fold where the "ears" end. Crease very sharply and unfold.

8 Open your paper and sink the right point inside the model by folding along the crease pattern shown.

9 Mountain-fold the model in half, bringing the bottom half up and behind the top half.

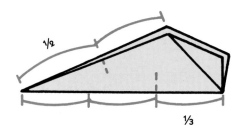

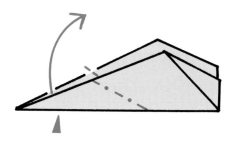

10 On the long top edge, make a pinch to mark the one-half point. On the long bottom edge, make a pinch to mark the one-third point as shown in the drawing.

11 Connect the dots: Make a valley fold that connects the two pinches you made in step 10. Fold and unfold.

12 Inside-reverse-fold the long point along the precrease made in step 11.

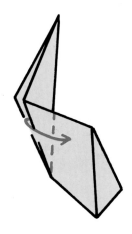

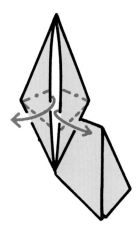

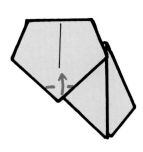

13 Open the model out to the right.

14 Following the crease pattern shown, open out the head and squash it flat into the shape shown in the next drawing.

15 Fold up a small triangle at the bottom of the head.

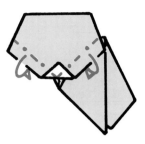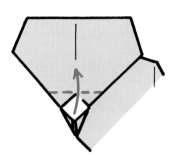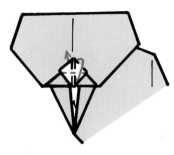

16 Mountain-fold the sides of the head behind as shown in the drawing.

17 Detail of the head: Fold up the tip of the nose.

18 Fold the tip down again, allowing the free corner to flip up at the same time.

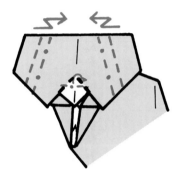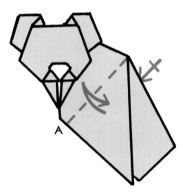

19 Blunt the tip of the nose. Pleat the ears back and then out again.

20 Mountain-fold the top edge of the head behind, accommodating near the ears by forming little triangles. (If it is easier for you, turn the model around to do this step.)

21 The loose points on the front and back will become the front legs of the Koala. Flip them up as far as they will go to create crease A. Then return them to their original position.

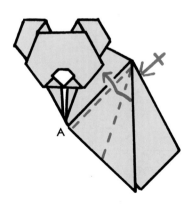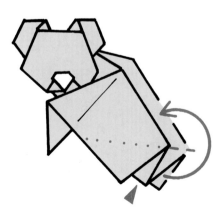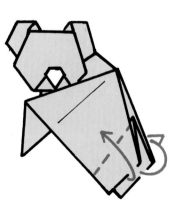

22 Bring the folded edge of the triangular flap to crease A, then refold on crease A. Repeat behind.

23 Inside-reverse-fold the central, hidden point at the Koala's bottom end.

24 Fold the short end up at the angle shown. Repeat on the other side.

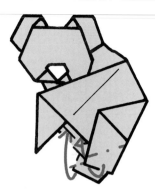

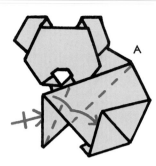

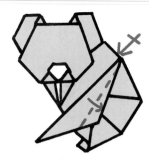

25 Mountain-fold the short edge so that it sits behind the second layer and in front of the hidden third layer. This forms the hind leg. Repeat behind.

26 Fold the front leg in half, then refold on crease A. Repeat on the other side.

27 Open out the paw into a long cup shape by folding on the crease shown. Repeat on the other side.

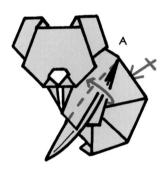

28 Refold the entire front leg on crease A. Repeat behind. The front legs will not lie flat because of the cup shape.

29 Mountain-fold the Koala's back inside the model. Repeat behind.

30 Your Koala is complete. The tension between the front legs will allow the Koala to clutch to your finger or a branch. Optional: To add dimensionality to the model, insert a finger between the layers of the Koala's back and press down on the ridge between the legs.

PEACOCK

Design by Adolfo Cerceda (Buenos Aires, Argentina)

★★★★
YOU SHOULD KNOW:

Waterbomb base
Inside reverse fold
Outside reverse fold
Squash fold
Rabbit ear

Watch the expression on people's faces as you lift and fan the train of this regal Peacock. This wonderful model was created by Adolfo Cerceda, known professionally as Carlos Corda. Born in Argentina, he toured the world entertaining audiences as a knife thrower.

In Cerceda's original model, the two halves of the tail were joined using glue. Subsequently, a clever lock, devised by English folder Paul Jackson, was incorporated into the sequence. This allows the model to be completed by folding alone.

PAPER:

Thin, crisp wrapping paper in the proportion of 2:1. A rectangle approximately 10″ × 20″ (25 × 50cm) is a good size. Do not use wrapping paper with glossy coating. If you do, the legs on the finished model will spread apart more than usual, giving you an awkward-looking model.

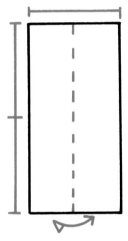

1 BOOK FOLD (mountain and valley) AND UNFOLD: Bring the long sides of the paper together, folding it in half. Crease and unfold. Turn your paper over and repeat this step on the other side to change the crease from a valley to a mountain.

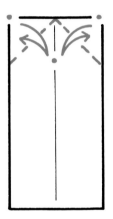

2 The white side of the paper is facing up. HOUSE-ROOF FOLD: Fold the top corners to the centerline. Crease and unfold.

3 Make the creases shown and then form a waterbomb base at the top half of the paper.

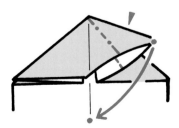

4 Lift up the right point until it is standing at a right angle to the rest of the model. Squash the flap down evenly. The centerline of the resulting kite shape should match the centerline of the rest of the paper.

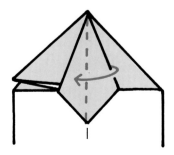

5 Turn the page: Fold the kite in half, bringing the right half over to cover the left half.

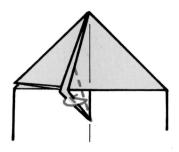

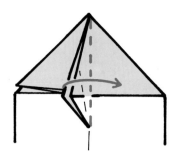

6 Fold the single raw edge to the folded edge. Crease and unfold.

7 Turn two pages to the right.

8 Fold the single raw edge to the folded edge. Crease and unfold.

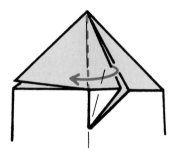

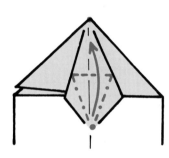

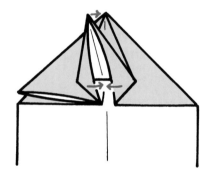

9 Turn one page to the left, bringing you back to your original kite shape.

10 As you lift the bottom point of the kite up to the top point . . .

11 . . . fold in on the existing creases to create a smaller, upside-down kite shape. This move is called a petal fold.

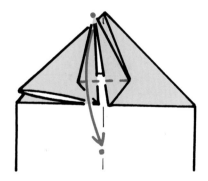

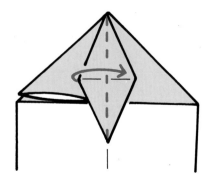

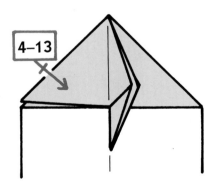

12 Fold the point down again, creasing through the widest part of the kite shape.

13 Fold the resulting diamond shape in half from left to right.

14 Repeat steps 4 through 13 on the left point. The result should look like drawing 15.

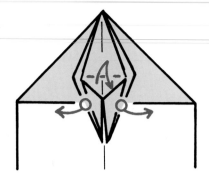

15 Flip the center tab up, make a sharp crease, and flip it down again. Then grasp the slender leg points. As you gently pull the leg points apart . . .

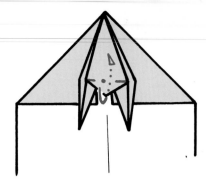

16 . . . push the center tab up inside the model to hide it and return the legs to their original position.

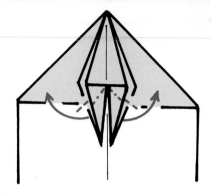

17 Inside-reverse-fold the legs out to the sides. (See the position they should take in the next drawing.)

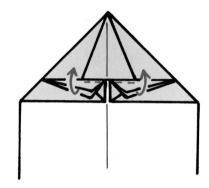

18 Notice that the horizontal folded edges are all aligned. Open the leg points by lifting the front flap of each.

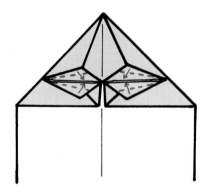

19 Narrow the legs by bringing the long sides almost to the centerline of each.

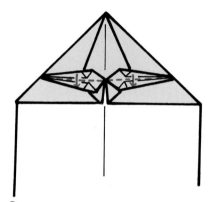

20 Fold the top half of each leg point over the bottom half.

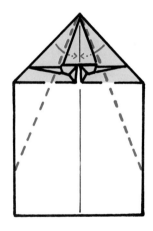

21 Bring the folded edges of the large triangle to the vertical centerline by slipping them under the legs and kite-shaped area of the model.

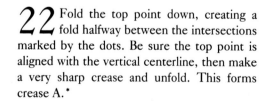

22 Fold the top point down, creating a fold halfway between the intersections marked by the dots. Be sure the top point is aligned with the vertical centerline, then make a very sharp crease and unfold. This forms crease A.*

*On smaller-size papers you will want to avoid having the pleated fan too close to the legs, so make fold A slightly closer to the lower dot. If you are folding the model from currency, fold A can be made right at the lower dot.

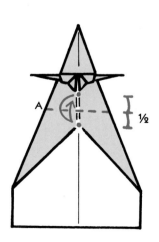

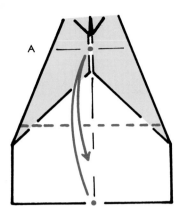

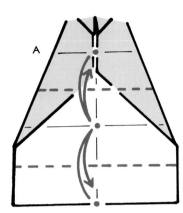

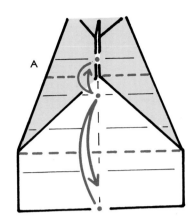

23 From crease A down is the tail area of the Peacock. It is formed by dividing the tail into sixteenths. First fold the tail in half: Bring the bottom edge up to crease A. Crease and unfold.

24 Fold the tail in quarters: Bring crease A to the one-half crease made in the last step. Match them carefully. (Also match the centerlines by turning to the back for a moment.) Crease sharply and unfold. Bring the bottom edge up to the one-half crease. Fold and unfold.

25 Fold the tail in eighths: Bring crease A to the nearest crease. Fold and unfold. Bring the bottom edge to the same one-quarter crease (now the third horizontal crease from the top). Fold and unfold.

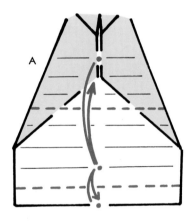

26 Fold the bottom edge up to the nearest crease. Bring crease A to the same crease. Crease sharply and unfold both folds.

27 The tail is now divided into eighths. Turn the paper over to the side that is all colored and divide the tail into sixteenths by putting a valley fold between each mountain fold. Pinch one of the tail creases up into a mountain fold and match this fold to the crease above it. Crease the valley between them. Unfold and repeat this procedure between every pair of mountain creases. Also fold the bottom edge to the nearest mountain crease. (Mountain and valley this crease only, leaving it as a valley fold.)

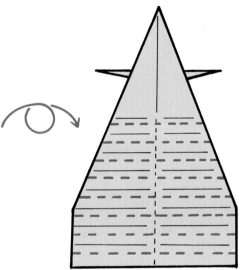

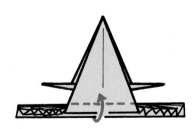

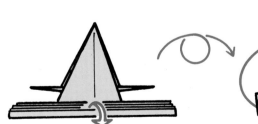

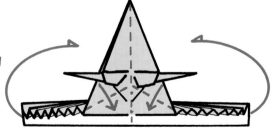

28 Along the existing creases, accordion-pleat the tail up to the position shown in the drawing. Grasp all of the pleats as a group and fold them up one more time along the valley-fold line shown.

29 Bring the raw edge down, unfolding the first pleat. Turn the model over.

30 Put in the creases shown. As the body section pops out into a rabbit ear, the tail section is mountain-folded in half and points backward.

91

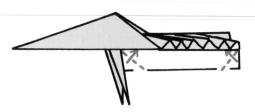

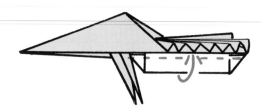

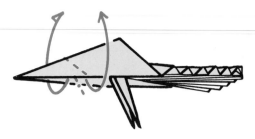

31 Lock the tail: Fold up the corners of the band that juts out below the tail—fold both layers together.

32 Fold the band up inside the nearest pleat of the tail. This will lock the two halves of the pleated tail together.

33 Outside-reverse-fold the long point up to the angle shown in the next drawing to form the Peacock's neck.

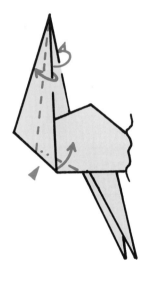

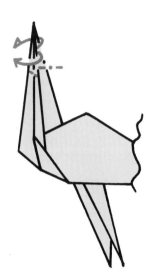

34 As you narrow the neck, a small triangle is formed at the bottom to accommodate for this fold. Repeat on the other side.

35 Head: Outside-reverse-fold the tip of the neck.

36 Pull the inner layers downward to enlarge the head to a kite shape. (You may find it easier to do steps 35 and 36 in one move.)

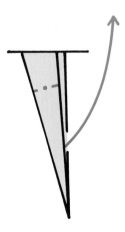

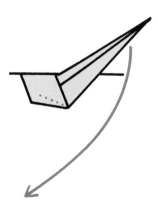

37 Pleat the tip of the head to form a beak.

38 Legs: Inside-reverse-fold the legs toward the tail.

39 Inside-reverse-fold the legs back down again.

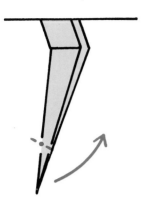 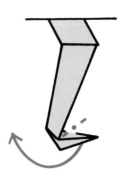 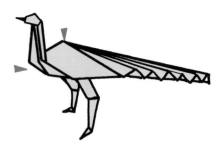

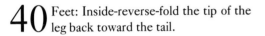

40 Feet: Inside-reverse-fold the tip of the leg back toward the tail.

41 Inside-reverse-fold the foot to the front.

42 Optional: Gently insert your thumbnail into the sharp points on the Peacock's back and chest to sink the points and blunt them slightly. (This is easiest to do by slightly spreading these areas apart before blunting, then reclosing them flat.)

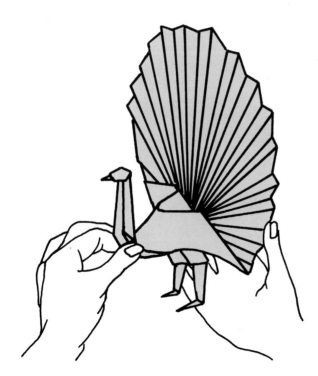

43 If the legs on your Peacock tend to spread apart, flatten the model under a heavy object or compress the beginning of the fan area between a clothespin and let the model rest for a day. If this doesn't work, use a little glue between the legs and the tail.

44 Your finished Peacock will stand by itself, and if its body is held and pressed gently upward from underneath the tail, it will spread its train of feathers for admirers.

Decorations

CHINESE LUCKY STAR

Traditional Design

★★
_____
PAPER:

A narrow strip approximately ½″ × 10″ (1.3 × 25cm) or of similar proportions. Foil paper will work well.

These five-pointed stars have recently become very popular in Hong Kong, where store owners leave a pile in a dish for shoppers to take. In Chinese tradition, the number five is lucky because it symbolizes the five happinesses: goodness, prosperity, longevity, propriety, and health.

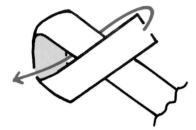 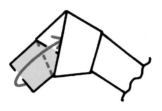 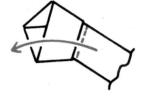

1 With the white side facing up, loosely tie the strip into a knot at the left end. The shape of the knot should form an even pentagon. Adjust the long and short tails accordingly.

2 Fold the short tail over the pentagonal-shaped knot. The short tail should not extend beyond the pentagon. If it does, snip or fold it a little shorter.

3 Fold the long tail over the short raw edge at one side of the pentagon and toward an opposite edge. Since a pentagon has an odd number of sides, an opposite side could be one of two sides. If you begin with a very even pentagon, the tail should naturally lean toward one of these two sides, and that will be your guide to tell you which direction to wind the tail.

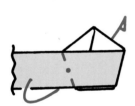 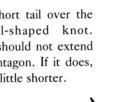  

4 Wrap the tail around the knot and toward an opposite side.

5 Continue wrapping the long tail around the pentagon in a manner that retains the even pentagon shape. As you wind the tail, make soft, not hard, creases to give the shape a slight puffiness.

6 Tuck the very end of the tail under the raw edge to lock it in place. If the tail is a little too long to do this, snip a little off and then tuck it under.

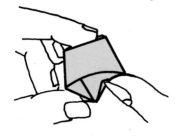

7 You should now have a multilayered, even pentagon-shaped "button." It is important that the shape be a little puffy and not completely flat. Hold the button between two fingers at the side edges. Do not hold the top and bottom surfaces. With your other hand, push in gently with your thumbnail at the center of one edge, causing it to indent inward. Repeat this step on all five sides to form a puffy star shape.

8 The finished Lucky Star.

To make a garland of stars:
Before you begin winding the tail around the pentagonal knot (step 3), lay a thin cord or thread over the knot and then proceed to wind the tail, enclosing the cord inside the star. Alternatively, you can use a needle and thread to string finished stars together.

FIVE-DIAMOND DECORATION

Design by Mike Thomas (Elgin, Illinois, USA)

This is one of many designs created by Mike Thomas, a member of CHAOS (CHicago Area Origami Society). This model makes a very nice decoration for a pin or barrette.

★ ★

YOU SHOULD KNOW:

Waterbomb base

PAPER:

A rectangle in the proportions 1:7. (To make a Three-Diamond Decoration use a 1:4 rectangle.) If you start with a slightly longer rectangle, you can cut off the excess when the model is complete. This will prevent you from running short of paper if your folding is not perfectly accurate.

This model can also be made from a United States dollar bill: Fold the bill lengthwise into thirds and then begin from step 1.

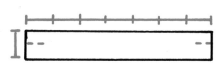

1 Begin with the white side facing up. Pinch the midpoint of each short side.

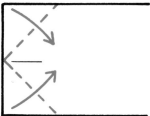

2 Fold the top and bottom left corners to the horizontal centerline.

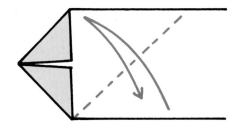

3 Fold the long bottom edge up to lie along the edges of the two small triangles. Crease and unfold.

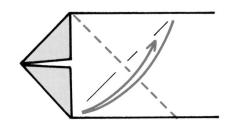

4 Repeat step 3, folding the top edge down and then unfolding.

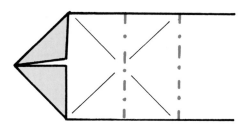

5 You should now see an **X** on your strip made up of two valley folds. Add a mountain fold at the vertical center of the **X** and at the right side of the **X**.

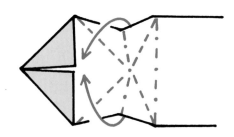

6 Push in on the mountain and valley folds of the **X** and form them into the shape of a waterbomb base, collapsing it to the left.

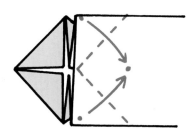

7 Fold the two new corners down to the horizontal centerline.

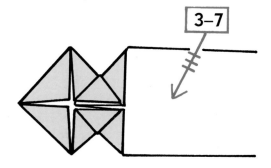

8 Repeat steps 3 through 7 three more times until your paper appears as in the next drawing.

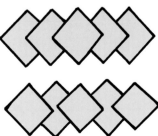

9 Fold the top and bottom right corners to the horizontal centerline. Then turn your model over.

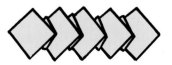

10 The Five-Diamond Decoration is finished.

Variations: By rearranging the folds, the diamonds can be formed into different patterns.

HEART LOCKET

Design by Gay Merrill Gross (New York, New York, USA)

This three-dimensional heart has an interior cavity for a small photo or secret message. It can be hung from a decorative cord and worn as a locket, or it can be used as a decoration on a gift. Folded from a large sheet, it can be used to enclose a small gift.

YOU SHOULD KNOW:

Inside reverse fold

PAPER:

Foil paper, origami paper, or gift wrap approximately 6″ (15cm) square. Skilled folders can make a heart from smaller-size squares.

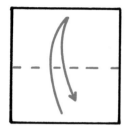

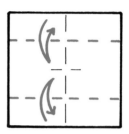

1 BOOKFOLD and UNFOLD: With the white side facing up, fold the square in half and unfold. Rotate the paper one quarter turn so that the center crease is now vertical.

2 Make a large PINCH at the center of the vertical crease.

3 CUPBOARD FOLD and UNFOLD: Bring the bottom and top edges inward to meet at the center pinch mark. Crease and unfold.

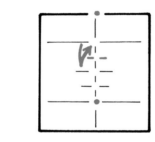
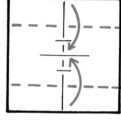

4 Match the dots: Bring the bottom edge up to the farthest crease, make a small pinch at the middle of the folded edge and unfold.

5 Match the dots: Bring the top edge down to the farthest crease, make a small pinch at the middle of the folded edge, and unfold.

6 Cupboard-fold on the existing creases.

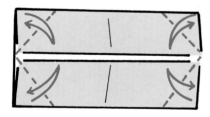
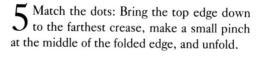
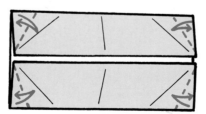
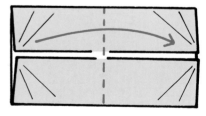

7 Fold each outside corner to the horizontal centerline. Crease sharply and unfold.

8 Fold in each corner so that the double raw edge lies on the nearest crease. Crease sharply and unfold.

9 BOOK FOLD: Bring the left side over to the right side, folding the paper in half. Then rotate the paper one quarter turn so that the folded edge is at the top.

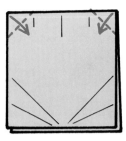

10 Using the two small pinch marks on the folded edge as a guide, fold the two top corners down to form two small triangles as shown in the next drawing.

11 Fold each half of the small top edge to lie along the vertical edge of the nearest small triangle. Make each fold separately; crease sharply and unfold.

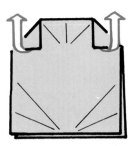

12 Unfold the two small triangles.

13 Fold each top corner so that the double-folded edge at the side lies along the nearest crease. Crease sharply and unfold.

14 Unfold the top folded edge.

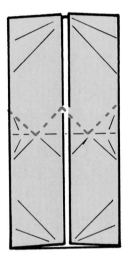

15 Change the four small creases shown to valley creases.

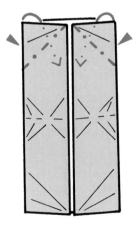

16 INSIDE REVERSE FOLD: Slightly separate the front and back layers of paper and push the top corners in between these two layers, folding on the existing creases.

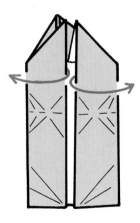

17 Separate the raw edges that meet in the center, slightly opening the "doors."

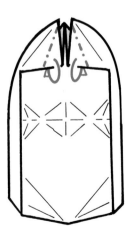

18 Narrow the interior triangular flaps by mountain-folding the edge of the flaps behind. You are folding on existing creases. Then reclose the "doors."

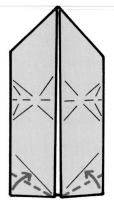

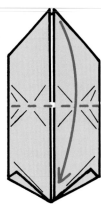

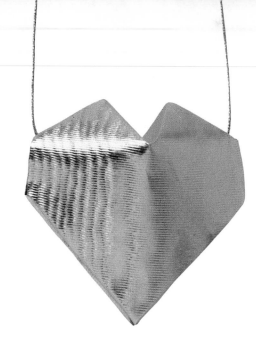

19 Fold up on the existing creases.

20 Fold the model in half from top to bottom.

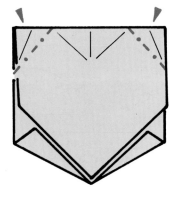

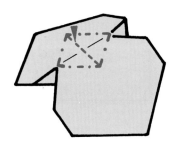

21 INSIDE REVERSE FOLD: Push the top corners between the front and back layers, folding on the existing creases.

22 View from top of model: Separate the front and back layers, then push down at the center of the top-folded edge. A diamond-shaped indentation should pop downward.

23 (Cutaway view.) Reach inside the model and narrow the two small triangular flaps by mountain-folding on the existing creases.

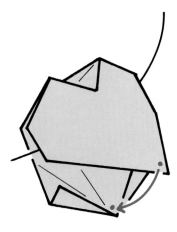

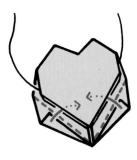

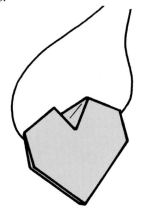

24 Insert a small photo, message, or object between the layers of the heart. Lay a decorative cord across the opening. Press the bottom points together to hold the heart closed.

25 Insert the side flaps of the back layer into the pockets of the top layer.

26 Completed Heart Locket.

HEXAHEDRON

Design by Molly Kahn (Nutley, New Jersey, USA)

★★

PAPER:

Three squares of equal size.

A simple but appealing origami model can be just as challenging to create as a complicated design. Molly Kahn is the creator of several simple but wonderfully effective designs.

A hexahedron is a three-dimensional shape with six sides or faces. This Hexahedron model is a modular made up of three identical units.

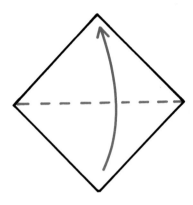

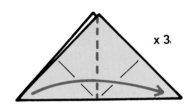

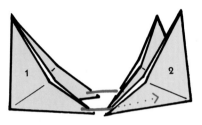

1 Begin with the white side facing up. DIAPER FOLD: Fold the bottom corner up to the top corner.

2 Fold the side points up to the top of the triangle. Crease sharply and unfold.

3 Fold the triangle in half, making a sharp crease. Repeat steps 1 through 3 on all three units.

4 Hold unit one so that the arms (two loose points) are at the bottom and point right. Hold unit two so the arms are at the right and point up. Insert the arms of unit one into the pockets (double layer on either side of the center crease) on unit two.

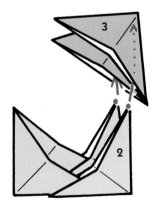

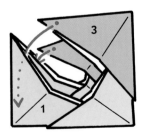

5 Hold unit three so that the arms are at the top and point left. Insert the arms of unit two into the pockets of unit three.

6 As you insert the arms of unit three into the pockets of unit one, open out the model so that it takes a three-dimensional shape.

7 Slide all three units together as far as possible and your Hexahedron is complete.

To hang: Insert a thread or wire before completely sliding all the units together. The model can be hung from either a wide point or a narrow point.

Ideas for Using the Hexahedron

These ideas come from John Blackman (Little Falls, New Jersey, USA), who specializes in creating uses for the origami models he folds.

Ornament: Hang the Hexahedron singly or hang several in graduated sizes.

Gift Box: A small gift, such as a piece of jewelry, can be enclosed inside the Hexahedron. For a see-through container, fold the units from sheets of plastic such as those used for report covers.

Pomander: Fill the Hexahedron with potpourri or spray cologne on a piece of cotton and enclose it in the model. Hang the pomander from a decorative cord.

Earrings: Make a pair of small Hexahedrons and hang them from thread or wire attached to an earring clip.

Necklace: As you string several Hexahedrons on a decorative cord, knot the cord before and after each "bead" to hold it in place.

Fortune Cookie: Write some humorous fortunes on little slips of paper and enclose each inside a Hexahedron. Add a small party favor if you wish.

Joined Hexahedrons

Half-a-Ball: Four Hexahedrons (twelve units) can be glued together to form a decorative shape with a flat bottom.

Magnet Decoration: Attach a magnet with self-adhesive backing (sold at craft supply stores) to the flat surface of the model. The model can now be used to hold notes and messages on metal surfaces such as refrigerator doors or file cabinets.

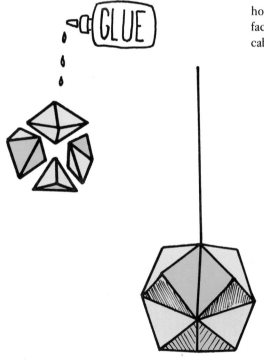

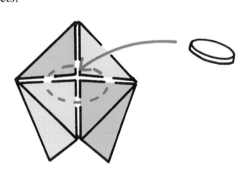

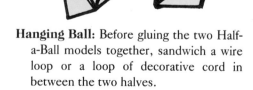

Hanging Ball: Before gluing the two Half-a-Ball models together, sandwich a wire loop or a loop of decorative cord in between the two halves.

Decorative Ball: Eight Hexahedrons (twenty-four units) can be glued together to form a ball taking the shape of a stellated octahedron. First form two Half-a-Ball models. Glue the two halves together, back to back.

FLUTED DIAMOND

Design by Molly Kahn (Nutley, New Jersey, USA)

Molly Kahn's first experience with folding came in the late 1920s, when she was a young child. To keep her occupied during a long illness, her mother bought her one of the very few books on paperfolding that were available then. Many years later, Molly's mother, Lillian Oppenheimer, became so enthusiastic about this enchanting pastime that in 1958 she founded the Origami Center of America.

The elegant shape of the Fluted Diamond makes a lovely ornament or bead for a necklace or earrings.

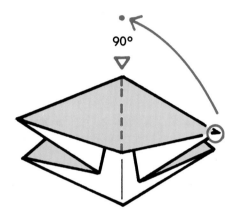

1 Begin with a preliminary base (see page 17) positioned so that the closed corner is away from you. Lift one flap from the right and swing it upward until it stands at a right angle to the rest of the paper.

2 SQUASH FOLD: Press down on the folded edge of the flap, causing the raw edges to spread apart.

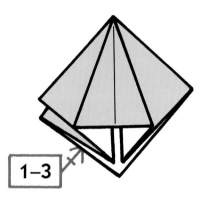

3 Flatten the flap into a tall triangular shape. Make sure the centerline of the tall triangle lies dead center by aligning it with the gap between the two small triangular "feet" below it. Turn your paper over and repeat steps 1 through 3 on the back.

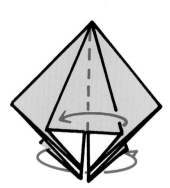

4 Turn the page: Flip the right half of the tall triangular shape over to the left. Turn the paper over and repeat.

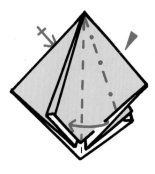

5 On the right you have exposed one of the full-size flaps from your original preliminary base. Repeat steps 1 through 3 on this flap, then turn the model over and repeat.

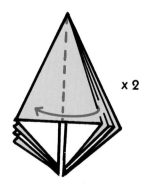

6 You have now squashed all four flaps of your original preliminary base. This completes one unit of your model. With your second square, make another unit, exactly the same as the first.

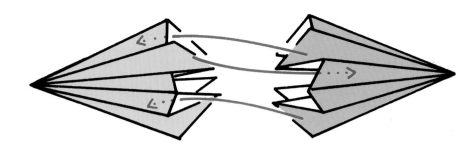

7 Looking at the top, closed end of each unit, spread the flaps away from each other, until all eight flaps are the same distance from each other.

8 To join the two units: Turn the units sideways and hold them so that the open ends face each other. Notice that the surface between two flaps either ends with a point (we will consider this a tab) or a raw edge (we will consider this a pocket). The tabs on one unit will be inserted into the pockets of the second unit and vice versa. This is a little tricky but not too difficult if you have a little patience.

HANGING ORNAMENTS

Many origami designs can be used to make decorative ornaments. Here are some basic techniques for hanging an origami model.

NEEDLE AND THREAD

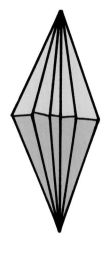

9 Slide the two units together as far as possible and arrange the flaps so that they are evenly spaced.

If you are going to hang this model as an ornament, you may wish to insert the thread, cord, or wire before joining the two units.

Single models: Put a needle and thread through the model and tie a small knot to hold the thread in place.

Multiple models: Use a long needle and strong thread and insert them through the entire model. Continue stringing the models on the same thread. Use a small button or bead, a small ornamental model, or a large knot at the beginning of the chain to prevent the models from slipping off.

WIRE LOOP

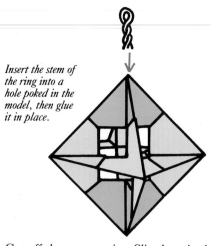

Insert the stem of the ring into a hole poked in the model, then glue it in place.

Bend a thin wire around a round stick or skewer to form a loop. Twist the two "tails" tightly together for approximately 1″ (2.5cm).

Cut off the excess wire. Slip the wire loop off the stick. Glue the twisted end of the wire into

the model. Thread a ribbon, cord, or thread through the loop and hang the model.

CORD

Method for Hanging Modulars:

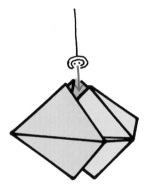

Fancy cords can add a decorative touch to your ornament. Try metallic cord, tassel cord, or thin ribbon. Thread or nylon fishing line will make your model appear to "float" in midair. A model hanging from thin elastic cord can add a bouncing effect. It is usually preferable to attach the cord before the model is complete.

1 Attach a "button" to the end of your cord. The "button" can be an actual small button, a sequin, a bead, a piece of crumpled aluminum foil, a small piece of a drinking straw, or a small scrap of paper.

2 Slightly separate some of the units on your modular and drop the "button" inside. Reclose the modular and hang the model from the cord.

Poked Hole Method:

1 Fold the model up to the base it is made from (or unfold it to this stage). Spread the base out to a half-open position and poke a hole through the center point of the paper with a pin or needle.

2 Also poke a hole through a tiny scrap of medium-weight paper.

3 Bend a very thin wire in half.

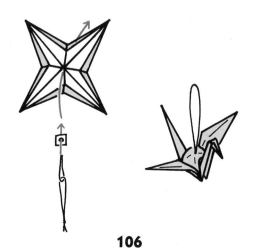

4 Tie the two ends of your cord together and slip the cord between the points of the wire.

5 Insert the wire through the hole in the paper scrap and pull the scrap down to the knot end of the cord.

6 Insert the wire through the inside of the base and pull the cord out the top of the base.

7 Slip the wire off the cord and complete the folding of the model.

JEWELRY

Origami models can be turned into unique, wearable jewelry. Customize your jewelry by choosing papers that match your wardrobe or your color scheme. Besides the origami models, you will need jewelry findings (such as earring wires, earring clips, pin backs, and barrette clips). These can be purchased in a craft or jewelry supply store. Depending on the model, you may want to give it a protective coating.

PINS and BARRETTES

Attach a flat origami model to the pin back or barrette clip using a strong adhesive such as a glue, craft or jewelry cement, or five-minute epoxy.

EARRINGS

Attach an eye pin or head pin (available at craft or jewelry supply stores) to your model by gluing it onto or inserting it through the model and bending a small loop at the end with round-nose pliers. If the pin is too long, it can be cut with wire cutters. Beads can also be added. Hook the loop at the end of the pin onto the earring wire or clip.

If you do not have eye pins or head pins, you can make a loop for hanging the model to the clasp by using strong thread and a needle or a very thin wire looped around a toothpick and twisted.

PROTECTIVE COATINGS

Clear Acrylic Spray. Spray the model outdoors or in a very well ventilated area. Several coats may be needed.

Nail Polish. Paint on clear nail polish. For a sparkly effect, use clear nail polish that comes with glitter in the bottle.

Acrylic Medium and Varnish. Such products come in gloss or matte finishes. Apply the varnish with a dampened brush. Several coats may be needed.

CORSAGE

Traditional Design

The flowers for this corsage are a traditional model. The flower arrangement was designed by Pearl Chin (New York, New York, USA). Pearl specializes in folding origami from beautiful Japanese *washi* papers. The corsage in the photograph shows off a type of *washi* paper that is dyed in variegated shades of the same color.

MATERIALS:

For the best result, use paper that is colored on both sides. You will need one 6″ (15cm) square for the leaf and several small squares (approximately 2″ [5cm] to a side) for the flowers. For the flower centers, you will need some small paper strips (colored on both sides) approximately $3/16″ \times 3/4″$ (0.4 × 2cm). To assemble the corsage, you will need thin florist wire and florist tape (both are available at craft stores or florist supply shops). Alternatively, you can use any thin wire and crepe-paper strips that can be wound around the wire with a little glue.

TOOLS:

Wire cutter and needle-nose pliers. If these are not available, try a pair of strong scissors and strong tweezers.

Flower:

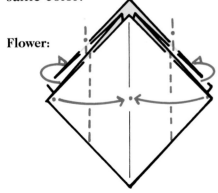

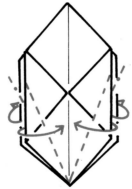

1 Begin with a preliminary base (see page 17) positioned as shown. If your paper is colored on only one side, reverse the color instructions for the preliminary base to give you a white base with a colored inside. Fold the side corners of the front layer to the center. Turn the paper over and repeat.

2 The open end of the paper should be away from you. Narrow the closed end by folding the lower edges of the front layer to the center. Turn the paper over and repeat.

3 Hold the stem end, then open the flower by pulling down on one of the top points. The flower should "blossom" open, showing four petals. Then pinch the stem end in half with a small mountain fold.

4 Your flower is complete and ready to be wired. If you wish, curl the tips of the petals with your fingers to curve them up or down.

1 With a wire cutter, cut a 6″ (15cm) length of thin florist wire for each flower. With needle-nose pliers, form a small loop at one end of the wire and insert one of the small strips. When the strip is centered, close the loop by pressing it between the broad end of the pliers.

2 Insert the bottom end of the wire into the flower and poke a hole through the bottom tip of the flower. Pull the wire down until a little of the flower center (the strip) sticks out between the petals.

3 Cut a short piece of florist tape from the roll (approximately 5″ [13cm] long) and stretch it slightly. (Stretching the florist tape releases the wax that enables the tape to stick to itself.) Beginning at the stem end of the flower, wrap the tape a few times around the base of the flower. This is done by holding the tape taut and slightly stretching it with one hand as you slowly twist the flower with your other hand.

4 After the stem end of the flower is covered with tape, slant the tape at a downward angle and continue twirling the wire as you hold the tape taut. Ideally, you want to pull the tape as tautly as you can without tearing it. Continue twisting the wire until the entire stem is covered. If there is any excess tape at the bottom, cut it off and pinch the bottom of the stem so that any loose tail of tape will stick to the rest of the tape.

When all of your flowers have centers and stems you are ready to assemble the Corsage.

Assembly:

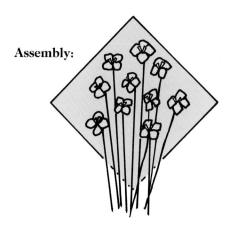

1 Place the large leaf square on the table so that one corner points toward you. Arrange the flowers on the leaf in a staggered fashion. When you are satisfied with the arrangement, pick up the wires of all the flowers at once, trying not to disturb the arrangement.

2 Approximately 1" (2.5cm) below the lowest flower, begin wrapping all of the stems together with a short piece of florist tape. Continue wrapping for a couple of inches, until all of the flowers are held together securely.

3 Now gather the bottom corner of the leaf square around the flower stems. When you are satisfied with the position of the leaf,

begin wrapping another piece of florist tape around the base of the leaf, attaching it to the flower stems. Continue wrapping the tape at a slanted angle until you have tightly wrapped all of the stems together and reached the bottom of the lowest stem.

4 Tie a ribbon into a bow at the base of the leaf and bend the end of the stems backward to hide it behind the flowers. Use a long straight pin to wear your Corsage, or use it as a decoration.

111

ORIGAMI FOR PARTIES

The colorful and playful shapes of origami make them a wonderful way to add a festive touch to a party. Here are ideas for using some of the models in this book.

INVITATIONS

Write your message directly on a flat origami model or attach the model to a card. Enclose the invitation in the Envelope model.

DECORATIONS

Prepare origami models as hanging ornaments by attaching a decorative cord. Drape a ribbon or cord across the room. Hang the origami ornaments from the ribbon using wire hooks, an unbent paper clip, or thread. As guests leave, remove an ornament and present it to each of them as a gift.

For a very dramatic effect, hang a large flock of Cranes individually from long ribbon or thread in varying lengths. Attach each ribbon to the ceiling or other high structure. In Hawaii, a thousand Cranes hung in this manner are often seen at celebratory occasions such as weddings and anniversaries.

CANDY CUPS

Fill the Basket model with nuts, candy, or other snacks.

HORS D'OEUVRE PICKS

Fold tiny origami models and glue them to the top of toothpicks.

PLACE CARDS

Write each guest's name on a card and use the Card Holder to stand the cards up at each place setting. If you are giving a dinner party, the Card Holder can be used to display the evening's menu.

PARTY FAVORS

Many of the action toys make delightful party favors to give away.

PARTY BAG

The Shopping Bag model makes a wonderful container for taking home party "loot."

PARTY ACTIVITY

Teach a simple origami design to your guests or demonstrate the spectacular "exploding" Butterfly Ball.

Look through other origami books for more ideas for origami toys and games, decorations, napkin folds, and flat models that can be attached to invitations.

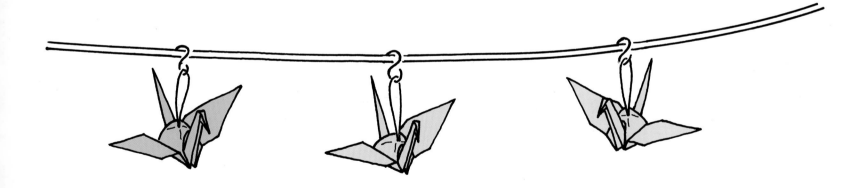

PART III

PAPERS AND SPECIAL TECHNIQUES

PAPER

Any paper that takes a crease well can be used for origami. A little experience will help you in choosing papers, but here are some guidelines to get you started.

The first and second time you fold a model it may not come out exactly right and you should consider these your practice models. Instead of wasting expensive, fancy papers on your learning models, look around for suitable "practice" paper. Practice paper should be inexpensive, but it should also be the right weight for that particular model. Bond paper is relatively inexpensive or free if you recycle flyers headed for the garbage. But the weight of this paper is better suited to a box or a picture frame. If you use it to fold a more intricate model, the thickness of the paper may produce an awkward-looking finished product and discourage you from trying the model again. Using a thinner paper may make the folding process easier, more satisfying, and the finished result a lot more pleasing. Packaged origami paper is usually an all-around good choice for

folding a model for the first time. New or used gift wrap has a similar weight and can also be used. Another option is onion-skin paper. When you are satisfied that you know the model well, you can start experimenting with fancier papers and search for the right ones to enhance the look of your model.

PACKAGED ORIGAMI PAPER

Thirty years ago if you asked for origami paper, you might be able to find square sheets, packaged in an assortment of rainbow colors. With the growth in the popularity of origami, the varieties of packaged origami paper have multiplied. Some of the "exotic" papers available include pearlescent, translucent, textured, foil paper, embossed foil paper, duo paper (a different color on each side), duo foil, shaded concentric circles, shaded stripes, shaded tips, and an endless variety of patterns and designs. Packaged papers have always been convenient to use because

they are precut into squares and are a suitable weight for most models. The numerous types now available make it easier to try out different kinds and find which one is best suited for an individual model.

WASHI PAPER

Washi paper is handmade paper from Japan. Some *washi* papers are solid colors, some have fibers running through them, some are decorated with a stencil technique, and some are printed with exquisite designs and patterns. The more decorative papers are very expensive, and *washi* paper is not usually easy to fold. It is a soft paper that does not hold or show a crease well. But in terms of strength, endurance, and appearance, *washi* paper has no equal and will create lasting, beautiful models.

FOIL PAPER

Foil papers add a bright look to your finished model, especially appropriate for stars and decorations. It also adds the advantage of allowing you to shape and mold the paper. On the other hand, it is not the paper to use if you are looking for a soft, subdued look. Crease lines are usually more obvious on foil paper, so avoid using it for designs where many precreases are used as guidelines, as these may mar the appearance of the finished model. Foil is also a poor choice for models where a spring action is desired (for instance, animals and toys that jump and hop).

GIFT WRAP

Most gift-wrap papers make an excellent choice for folding. Best of all, they come in an extensive array of colors and patterns. Avoid gift wrap with a glossy coating as these papers do not hold a crease well and may also crack along fold lines.

MONEY

The most expensive of all folding papers is money, but paper currency is printed on very strong, high-quality paper, and models folded from it have added appeal and make wonderful gifts. Use it to fold designs that are made from rectangles such as the Shirt and Pants, the Five-Diamond Decoration, or for excellent folders, the Peacock.

FREE PAPER

While paper is relatively inexpensive compared to most art and craft materials, it need not cost even a penny! Tons of paper are thrown away every day and some can be recycled into wonderful origami models. Here are some suggestions for using some of these papers:

Flyers. Frequently printed on bright-colored bond paper to attract the readers' attention, this paper can be used to fold models that can be made from medium-weight paper. (Try Boxes, Basket, Stellated Octahedron, Pop-up Snake, Hexahedron, Butterfly Bomb.)

Magazine covers and calendars. These make wonderful, sturdy boxes.

Magazine pages. Because magazine pages have a glossy coating and do not hold a crease well, a finished model may tend to unfold and spread a little. On certain models where the folds are fairly well locked on completion, however, magazine pages do work. You can take advantage of some very pretty and colorful designs found in magazines, but keep in mind that magazine pages are not ideal for learning a new model. The creases are not seen as well as on solid-colored, uncoated papers. (Try Crane, Boxes, Shopping Bag, Stellated Octahedron, Magic Pocket, Lucky Star.)

Wallpaper and wallpaper sample books. Look for the kind that is all paper or has a paper backing. Do not use vinyl wallcovering, as this will not hold a crease. (Try Boxes, Hexahedron.)

Plastic sheets. Plastic, such as see-through report covers, is not easy to fold, but some models can be made from this material if you make supersharp creases (use a folding tool such as a letter opener to help you). (Try Hexahedron, Fluted Diamond, Crane.)

Here are some more sources of free folding papers:

Computer paper	Leftover florist paper
Stationery	Paper bags
Used envelopes from greeting cards	Decorative shopping bags
Foil linings from envelopes	Posters
Business envelopes with an interesting pattern on the inside	Maps
Leftover gift wrap	Shelf paper

SPECIAL TECHNIQUES

DECORATING PAPERS

Akira Yoshizawa, the great Japanese origami master, folds from papers made to his specifications. In the United States, origami artist Michael LaFosse makes his own handmade papers for his folded designs. You may not want to go as far as these two artists, but you may want to do something to individualize the papers you fold and make them uniquely your own. By employing various decorating and laminating techniques, you can take what is already available and customize it to suit the specific model you are doing.

Webbing. To add an irregular "webbed" pattern to your paper, webbing can be purchased in a spray can and is available at craft and art supply stores. Use it in a well-ventilated area.

Rubber Stamps. Buy commercially made stamps or make your own using a white plastic eraser and linoleum carving tools. Cut out geometric patterns or other shapes and then decorate the paper using your stamp and a stamp pad.

Sponge Painting. Cut a sponge into smaller rectangles and drop liquid watercolor or pearlescent colors onto a dampened piece of sponge. Print or stroke the color onto sturdy paper (the white side of foil paper will work well).

Speckling. Dip a small brush in liquid watercolor. Tap the brush against your finger for a spray of colored specks on your paper. Use plenty of newspaper!

Photocopier Designs. If you find a design or pattern you like, you can replicate it in black and white by using a photocopier machine. For special effects, enlarge the pattern or move the original on the glass as you copy it for a swirl effect.

Computer Designs. Create a design on your computer and print it. The original can be used as a master and replicated on a photocopier.

Laminating Paper. Use glue, bookbinder's paste, or adhesive spray mount (in a well-ventilated area) to adhere two sheets together, back to back.

SOURCES FOR ORIGAMI MATERIALS

Origami USA (formerly known as The Friends of The Origami Center of America) offers a complete selection of origami books as well as a wide variety of packaged origami papers. All books and paper must be ordered by mail. For a supplies list, send a self-addressed envelope with two first-class stamps to

Origami USA
15 West 77th Street
New York, NY 10024-5192

STORES

Japanese bookstores and gift shops frequently carry packaged origami paper. Some Japanese food stores also carry this paper.

Some art supply stores may carry *washi* paper, marbleized paper, or packaged origami paper.

The following is a list of stores in major U.S., Australian, and Canadian cities and the paper they carry.

B—Origami books
M—Marbleized paper
P—Packaged origami paper
W—*Washi* paper

Chicago

Aiko's Art Materials Import, Inc.
3347 North Clark Street
Chicago, IL 60657
(312) 404-5600
B, M, P, W

Denver

Kobun-Sha
1255 19th Street
Denver, CO 80202
(303) 295-1845
B, P

Los Angeles

Kinokuniya Bookstore
123 Onizuka Street, Suite 205
Los Angeles, CA 90012
(213) 687-4480
B, P

Melbourne Area

Japan Mart
568 Malvern Road
Prahran, Victoria
Australia
510-9344
P

McGills Authorised Newsagency
187 Elizabeth Street
Melbourne, Victoria
Australia
602-5566
P

New York City Area

New York Central Art Supply
62 Third Avenue
New York, NY 10003
(212) 473-7705   (800) 950-6111
M, P, W

Kate's Paperie
561 Broadway
New York, NY 10012
(212) 941-9816
M, P, W

Kinokuniya Bookstore
10 West 49th Street
New York, NY 10020
(212) 765-1461
B, P, W

Yaohan Plaza
595 River Road
Edgewater, NJ 07020
(201) 941-7580
Yaohan Food Store—P
Kinokuniya Bookstore—B

Zen Oriental Bookstore
521 Fifth Avenue
New York, NY 10175
(212) 697-0840
B, P

Orlando (EPCOT Center)

Mitsukoshi
Japan Pavilion—EPCOT Center
P.O. Box 10000
Lake Buena Vista, FL 32830
(407) 827-8513
B, P

San Francisco

Kinokuniya Bookstore
1581 Webster Street
San Francisco, CA 94115
(415) 567-7625
B, P

The Paper Tree
1743 Buchanan Mall
San Francisco, CA 94115
(415) 921-7100
B, P, W

Seattle

Uwajimaya
6th South & South King
Seattle, WA 98104
(206) 624-6248
B, P

Toronto

The Japanese Paper Place
887 Queen Street West
Toronto, Ontario M6J 1G5
Canada
(416) 369-0089
B, M, P, W

ORIGAMI SOCIETIES

Most origami societies sell origami books and paper, hold classes and conventions, and publish a magazine of diagrams and origami-related articles. They welcome folding enthusiasts of any age or level, from beginning to experienced. Here is a listing of some of the larger national groups.

ARGENTINA
Origamistas Argentinos
Gorostiaga 1588
1426 Buenos Aires
Argentina

AUSTRALIA
Australian Origami Society
2/5 Broome Street
Highgate
Perth 6000
Australia

BELGIUM
Belgisch-Nederlandse Origami Societeit
Postbus 49
B-2440 Geel
Belgium

BRAZIL
Centro Brasileiro de Difusao de Origami
R. Honorio Libero 154
01445 São Paolo
Brazil

CANADA
For information on Canadian origami societies, contact Origami USA. The staff there will be happy to tell you how to contact origami groups in your area.

DENMARK
Dansk Origami Center
Ewaldsgade 4, KLD
2200 Copenhagen-N
Denmark

ENGLAND
British Origami Society
11 Yarningale Road
Kings Heath
Birmingham B14 6LT
England

FRANCE
Mouvement Français des Plieurs de Papier
56 rue Coriolis
75012 Paris
France

GERMANY
Origami Deutschland e.V.
Postfach 1630
8050 Freising
Germany

Origami München
Postfach 22 13 24
8000 München 22
Germany

HOLLAND
Origami Societeit Nederland
Postbus 35
9989 ZG Warffum
The Netherlands

ISRAEL
Israel Origami Art Society
Mevo Ha'Asara 1/22
Jerusalem 97876
Israel

ITALY
Centro Diffusione Origami
Casella Postale 42
21040 Caronno Varesino
Italy

JAPAN
Nippon Origami Association
1-096 Domir Gobancho
12 Gobancho, Chiyodaku
Tokyo 102
Japan

SPAIN
Asociación Española de Papiroflexia
María Guilhou, 2-3°-C
28016 Madrid
Spain

U.S.A.
Origami USA
15 West 77th Street
New York, NY 10024-5192
USA

INDEX